The Joy of Classical Music

JOAN KENNEDY

The Joy of Classical Music

A Guide for You and Your Family

NAN A. TALESE

DOUBLEDAY

New York   London   Toronto   Sydney   Auckland

PUBLISHED BY NAN A. TALESE
an imprint of Doubleday, a division of
Bantam Doubleday Dell Publishing Group, Inc.
666 Fifth Avenue, New York, New York 10103

DOUBLEDAY and the portrayal of an anchor
with a dolphin are trademarks of
Doubleday, a division of Bantam Doubleday Dell
Publishing Group, Inc.

Library of Congress Cataloging-in-Publication Data

Kennedy, Joan Bennett.
The joy of classical music: a guide for you and your family
Joan Kennedy.—1st ed.
p.   cm.
Includes bibliographical references and index.
1. Music appreciation.   I. Title.
MT6.K355J7   1992
781.6'8—dc20   92-12028
CIP
MN

ISBN 0-385-41262-2
Printed in the United States of America
November 1992
First Edition

1   3   5   7   9   10   8   6   4   2

For
Kara and Michael
Teddy Jr.
and
Patrick

ACKNOWLEDGMENTS

FOR HER INVALUABLE ASSISTANCE in helping me prepare this manuscript for publication, I give my heartfelt thanks to Heidi Waleson, a fellow music lover and writer. I've enjoyed a wonderful working relationship with John Williams, who has conducted me with his orchestra, the Boston Pops, at Symphony Hall and at the annual free outdoor July 4th concerts in Boston, and I thank him for contributing his Foreword. I also owe thanks to the late Leonard Bernstein, who, ten years ago, was the first to encourage me to write this book. Yo-Yo Ma, the world-renowned cellist and my longtime Boston pal, offered freely of his advice and wisdom, for which I am grateful. Thanks also to: Sandi Nicolucci, who coached me through the year of teaching music to kindergarten through eighth grade that was required for my master's degree in education, providing me with experiences that were useful in writing this book; Leontyne Price, the great soprano, who shared with me her view of the world of opera; and Bruce Marks, Artistic Director of the Boston Ballet and a dear friend, who helped enormously with the material on ballet. Finally, I want to thank my editor and fellow Manhattanville College alumna, Nan A. Talese, for her guidance and enthusiasm; our days together in college no doubt contributed to the atmosphere of trust that allowed me to write this book.

CONTENTS

CONTENTS

FOREWORD

I'VE KNOWN JOAN KENNEDY for more than a decade now, and I can't think of a better person to communicate the pleasures of music to people who want to learn more about it. In her wonderful new book—a charming mix of personal history, musical lore, practical suggestions, and behind-the-scenes peeks at musicians and their lives—her love of music leaps from the page, inviting novices and experienced listeners alike to join in.

The Joy of Classical Music deals with some fascinating questions. Why do we listen to music, and what do we hear in it? How much do we understand about this phenomenon which is so truly a human need, and so basic a form of expression?

All through the ages and in every culture, dances of joy, drums of war, and songs of love, celebration, and sorrow have formed an indispensable part of our social and religious life. The music we hear speaks of those thoughts and feelings that cannot be expressed in language, but which can be felt, recognized, and understood by all of our fellow human beings.

Leonard Bernstein wrote that "all music is one." Ethnic, folk, pop, jazz, rock, symphonic, vocal, instrumental, religious, secular—music shares our common humanity as its basis. The variety of music is infinite, and it would take several lifetimes to study, learn, and appreciate all of its rich forms. At the higher artistic levels, music is considered a civilizing force, and as such, it is necessary for young people as part of their general education. Yet as Joan shows us, it is easy to begin to love and understand music, and with an overview such as this, we gain the tools to begin to understand it all.

This sense of the oneness of music has fueled my years with the Boston Pops. We offer our audience a chance to sample classical music on programs that include more familiar idioms, such as popular, jazz, and folk forms. Like other pops orchestras, we try to make connections among all these different kinds of music, tracing the broad sources of folk music that have been forged into what we call "art" music, and we have fun doing it. Pops concerts provide quality symphonic music to listeners who think they might be uncomfortable with a classical concert, and as such, these concerts are a wonderful entree into that world.

Leonard Bernstein, one of the most eloquent voices on this subject in both music and speech, used to speak of "the joy of music." Joan Kennedy celebrates this spirit as she writes movingly and lovingly about the art she knows so well, and she gives us the means to discover this joy for ourselves.

JOHN WILLIAMS
Boston, Massachusetts
February 1992

AUTHOR'S INTRODUCTION

*I must study politics and war that my sons may have the liberty
to study mathematics and philosophy . . . in order to give their
children the right to study painting, poetry and music.*
                                          —President JOHN ADAMS

EARLY in 1990, my only daughter Kara, then age thirty,
told me that she and her boyfriend Michael were engaged to
be married. We settled on a September date and started planning the Hyannis Port wedding. Among all of the issues and
details to be discussed, researched, and resolved, the one clos-
est to my heart was the music.

I had some ideas, and so did Kara. She was absolutely
adamant about one of them: she wanted a gospel choir performing at the church. I was dubious. My background is
classical music, and that's the music I expected at the wedding. I knew nothing about gospel, and I couldn't imagine
how it would fit into a Roman Catholic service. But it was
Kara's wedding, and she wanted it, so I went off to find out
something about this music, to do some "sleuthing," as Kara
put it. All that spring, I went to churches in Boston to see
what I could find, and the more I heard, the more I liked.
On September 8, when the five hundred guests got to Our
Lady of Victory Church in Centerville, Massachusetts, the

first sounds they heard were thirteen singers and a jazz pianist from the Twelfth Baptist Church in Roxbury.

Those singers gave the Eucharistic Celebration and Rite of Marriage of Kara Kennedy to Michael Allen a swinging beat and a transcendent spirit that I could never have imagined. They sang a half-hour "concert" before the ceremony, a stirring "Alleluia" after the Gospel, a jazzed-up version of the Catholic hymn "They Will Know We Are Christians by Our Love," and a serene "Let There Be Peace on Earth" as part of the Sign of Peace. When Kara and Michael had placed wedding rings on each other's hands, the singers burst into a swinging rendition of "O Happy Day" that had the whole twenty-eight-member bridal party—and the congregation—swaying along. And for the recessional, the chorus teamed up with the Concordia Brass Quintet for one of the most amazing renditions of Beethoven's "Ode to Joy" that I have ever heard. As Kara and Michael posed for the press photographers on the church steps, this ebullient music wafted out of the church, giving them a high-stepping sendoff.

My friends couldn't believe it. They assumed that if Joan Kennedy were planning a wedding, the music would be a string quartet from the New England Conservatory playing Mozart in the balcony. But they loved it, and so did I. And I think what I loved most about it was that my daughter gave me a tip about something I knew nothing about, gave me the impulse and motivation to learn, and the result was not only a great success, but an emotional charge. I knew a lot about one kind of music, but I found that it was pretty easy—and pretty exciting—to find out about another.

Classical music has been central to my life since my childhood, and it became my identifying trait when I married into the Kennedy family. As I traveled all over the United States, campaigning for my brothers-in-law as they ran for President in 1960 and 1968, people would ask me about music. After speeches, at parties, and at fundraisers, after I had played "The Star-Spangled Banner" or "This Land Is Your Land" on the piano for the hundredth time, people would approach me to ask how they could learn about classical music. When should their children start piano lessons? they wanted to know. What composers should they listen to? In 1980, when my husband Ted was running for President, they were still asking me those questions, and people I meet today are too.

These people yearn for something. They believe that classical music could enrich their lives, but they are intimidated by it. They assume that symphonies and operas are for people who grew up listening to them and therefore have some sort of innate understanding of that sort of music. They assume that such music is inaccessible, difficult, and expensive. They say they couldn't possibly go to the ballet or the opera or the symphony or jazz concerts because they don't know anything about it, which is like saying you can't go to a baseball game because you don't know all the rules and you don't know where the stadium is or how much the tickets cost.

I'm not sure how classical music acquired this kind of mystique. Certainly it wasn't that way when much of the music of the past was written: everyone in Italy rushed to the opera houses to hear Giuseppe Verdi's latest when it came out, just as everyone today goes to the latest movie or tunes in a popular television show.

Classical music isn't strange and foreign. Look around: it's in the air. Adults who grew up with Saturday morning cartoons heard Jacques Offenbach's *Orpheus in the Underworld* as they watched Farmer Gray chase marauders out of his garden, and they knew the overture to Gioacchino Rossini's opera *William Tell* (dah-dah-dum, dah-dah-dum, dah-dah-dum-dum-dum) as the galloping hooves of the Lone Ranger's horse. Anyone who has heard the musical *Kismet* and its famous song "Stranger in Paradise" knows Alexander Borodin's *Prince Igor:* the songs were built on its melodies. Remember the song "Tonight We Love"? It's the first big theme from Tchaikovsky's Piano Concerto No. 1. At the ballet, you hear the music of great composers as you watch the dancers onstage. The nineteenth-century composer Tchaikovsky created the music for *Swan Lake* and *The Nutcracker;* George Balanchine, perhaps the greatest choreographer of our century, saw dances in the music of one of his greatest composer contemporaries, Igor Stravinsky.

Classical music resounds through movie theaters. Richard Strauss's monumental tone poem *Also sprach Zarathustra* is the menacing, mysterious background to the classic *2001: A Space Odyssey.* The yearning melodies from Giacomo Puccini's operas *La Rondine* and *Gianni Schicchi* give musical depth to a young girl's awakening to love and life in *A Room with a View.* The movie *Amadeus* splashed on the screen the tumultuous career of Mozart, child prodigy, musical genius, and brilliant composer of the eighteenth century. Maurice Ravel's *Boléro* got a new lease on life as the erotic leitmotif of the movie *10.* On television, advertising agencies use classical melodies to sell everything from luxury cars and airlines to bug spray, painkillers, hamburgers, and soft drinks. Corporations play classical music while you are on hold on the phone; restaurants offer discreet backgrounds of Baroque trios. This music is not hard to listen to. It is neither arcane nor inaccessible, but a part of everyday life.

Classical music *is* second nature to me, and it touches my emotions at a much deeper level than any other art. It is joyous, exciting, stimulating, even erotic; it is also troubling and saddening. Music is about loss, celebration, triumph. Yo-Yo Ma, the wonderful cellist, who speaks so eloquently in words as well as music, once said to me, "Every single emotion can be found in music, and once you open up to it, it's hard to close yourself off again to things around you. It makes you feel more alive."

But you needn't have listened to Brahms at age four or have a degree in musicology to feel that way, and you're never too young or too old to start. It helps to know what the terms mean and who the composers are, but not even that is essential. The thing to remember is that you can become a musical gourmet just by listening. All you have to do is open your mind to it—to take the risk, just as I did with those gospel singers at my daughter's wedding.

This book is about how to start taking those steps. It is a practical guide that begins with my own experiences discovering music for myself and with my own children and friends. The book then broadens to include suggestions on how anyone, regardless of income or geography, can do the same. I'll talk about techniques that worked with my children, nieces and nephews, and friends, about listening to and participating in musical activity at home, in school, at performances. I'll demonstrate how much music of various kinds exists where you might least expect it, and how to go about finding it. I'll also offer a basic introduction to musical terms, composers, and works.

Although I learned about music not to be a professional, but for pleasure, music for me isn't a frill; it's central. I can't resist quoting Yo-Yo Ma again. Yo-Yo spends his life rushing in and out of airports all over the world, dragging his baggage and his cello in its heavy case, staying up late, missing his wife and his two children, but music makes it worth it. He says, "Life is so pressured today that we all feel guilty about not doing enough, and we don't often let our imaginations go freely to a pleasant spot. We become so goal-oriented that all we do is think about goals and forget to live. Think about living as taking a trip to the top of a mountain. How are you going to take that trip? Are you going to drive ninety miles an hour to get there in as straight as possible a path? Or are you going to take a country road, stop for a leisurely lunch, pick a lot of flowers, and then get there and feel you're on top of the world? The second way—that's music."

The Joy of Classical Music

ONE

Growing Up
with Music

THE RADIO stood at the center of the house in Bronxville, New York, where I grew up in the 1940s and 1950s. As you came through the front door into the entrance hall between the living room and the dining room, you would see it at the foot of the staircase: a massive console with a turntable perched on top. Like the piano in the living room, it was a fixture, an unchanging piece of furniture, and it was almost always on. Concerts of the New York Philharmonic, live from Carnegie Hall, wafted up the circular stairway to the bedroom where I was doing my homework, and the insistent "Dah-Dah-Dah-DAH" of Beethoven's Fifth Symphony distracted me from my math problems. On Saturday afternoons, the voices of Metropolitan Opera sopranos and tenors reached back to the kitchen and out to the garden. In the evenings, my mother turned off the radio and stacked 78 rpm records on the turntable to accompany our supper. Stacking records was usually forbidden—it scratched them—but at four minutes per side, it took a lot of 78s to get through a Chopin piano concerto and make an uninterrupted meal, so my mother reluctantly gave in to convenience.

The radio and the phonograph were our at-home entertainment. Television didn't appear until I was in high school, when we were one of the first families in the neighborhood to acquire one, a tiny black and white model. We bought one because my father, an advertising executive, needed to watch the Colgate and Palmolive shampoo and soap ads. With the television, though, programming was limited, unlike music, which seemed limitless.

Music was a part of life for my parents. Harry and Virginia (Ginny) Bennett didn't play instruments very well or attend many concerts, but they loved all kinds of music. If the radio wasn't on, Ginny was singing. It might be a tune from a Sigmund Romberg operetta (I can still hear her warbling "My desert is waiting") while she straightened up the living room, or hits from the thirties—her teenage heyday— like Cole Porter's "Night and Day" or "Begin the Beguine" as she got dressed to go out in the evening. Music had an emotional charge for Ginny, whether it was George Gershwin's songs or the operas of the great Italian composer Giuseppe Verdi. I picked up her feeling just from being around her and her music, and my tastes became catholic too.

I was born on September 2, 1936, the oldest of two daughters. I was named for my mother, Virginia Joan Bennett, but my parents called me Joan so as not to have the confusion of two Ginnys in the house. I called them Harry and Ginny—it was what they called each other, and they never suggested I do anything different. Most of the families in our New York City suburb had fathers who commuted to Manhattan and mothers who stayed at home, and ours was no exception:

every day my father took the twenty-four-minute train ride to Madison Avenue, and when my sister and I came home from school, my mother was there to greet us.

Cultural accomplishments were considered de rigueur for little girls in Bronxville. I suppose it was a throwback to nineteenth-century ideals of gracious living, when all young ladies did a little playing or drawing. Live music as entertainment at home had already pretty much given way to the record player and the radio, but all my friends took piano or ballet lessons, so at age five, I made my first pilgrimage to the neighborhood piano teacher.

Maud Perry was every child's nightmare authority figure: imposingly plump, gray-haired, and strict, with a big, ugly straw hat with flowers on it that she wore on special occasions, like student recitals. She terrified me, and I knew right away that she meant business. There was no physical punishment, no rapping of knuckles or anything like that, but the silent, disapproving stare when my lesson was not well prepared, and the knowledge that all she had to do was mention my slackness to my mother for that disapproval to continue at home, were enough to ensure my diligence.

Once a week after school I walked the few blocks to Miss Perry's house. It was like a factory: pupils started coming at three, and every half hour until seven-thirty a new one arrived. I would wait in her front hall with its overstuffed chairs and tasseled lampshades, listening as the student ahead of me stumbled or sailed through his or her piece, wondering if I sounded that bad—or that good. Then the student would pack up her music and depart, and it was my turn.

Those early lessons began with lots of exercises. Scales and arpeggios (chords played one note at a time) in all the different keys got my fingers moving around the keyboard, and the sound of music's building blocks into my head. Most children claim to hate scales, but I always liked them. You don't have to be terribly gifted to be good at them, and you don't have to worry about phrasing or expression when you're working on them—what counts is finger dexterity. Mastering exercises gives an instant sense of accomplishment, which I think is great for kids. Also, once your fingers know those scales, they don't forget—it's like riding a bicycle. To this day, when I'm nervous, fidgety, or bored, sitting in a cab or a plane, or trying to fall asleep, I drum out arpeggios with my fingers. It's my way of releasing tension, or counting sheep.

At first I played simple pieces written especially for beginners—short tunes with pictorial titles like "My Little Wooden Shoes." When I was ten, I graduated to simplified versions of the great works. This form of teaching is out of fashion now—purists feel that children should be exposed to music as it was written, and certainly there is plenty of music by the great composers that is suitable for children at all levels of accomplishment. Still, it was tremendously exciting to play sections of the nineteenth-century piano concertos (big pieces for piano and orchestra) by Frédéric Chopin (1810–49), Johannes Brahms (1833–97), and Sergei Rachmaninoff (1873–1943) which I had heard on the radio, or on my parents' records.

The arrangements usually had just the melody in the right hand with a simple accompaniment in the left. I knew what the real thing sounded like, though. Those big concertos thunder and roar as the piano soloist, seated at the long black concert grand at the front of the stage, does sonic battle with the huge orchestra behind, and the conductor, standing between them, holds it all together. I used to plunge into the first movement of the First Piano Concerto of Piotr Ilyich Tchaikovsky (1840–93)—which I also knew, of course, as the song "Tonight We Love"—and feel as though that orchestra was about to come in at any moment. I never did play the great Romantic concertos in their real versions, but when I listen to them now, I have a physical and emotional reaction: I just know how it would feel.

The unabridged repertoire I worked on was usually from the Baroque (seventeenth and early eighteenth century) and Classical (eighteenth and early nineteenth century) periods. Sonatinas, just a page or two long, by Muzio Clementi (1752–1832), perhaps, were melodic and not too complicated, and a good precursor to the more elaborately worked out sonatas of Franz Joseph Haydn (1732–1809) and Wolfgang Amadeus Mozart (1756–91) that came next. So much of the music of those eras is based on dance rhythms, which was also fun for me, since I always loved dancing. Composers like Antonio Vivaldi (1678–1741) and Mozart have a special buoyancy to their music which comes from those dances— you can almost see the steps.

The music of Johann Sebastian Bach (1685–1750) appealed to me for some of the same reasons that I liked exercises. It was straightforward; even though the preludes, fugues, and inventions could be quite complicated, they were logical, and it was a challenge to have to play two entirely different lines at the same time. A melody, or scrap of a melody, would start in the right hand. Then it would move to the left hand, and then both hands would play it together—though not quite in synch. You also played the theme backward and varied it in a half-dozen ways, and at the climax, both hands would play together and get louder, which always told me that the ending was just ahead. I liked the tension and movement of the two musical lines working against each other; it was an intellectual as well as a physical challenge.

My Bach pieces were usually short, which made them easy to memorize, a feature I liked a lot. They also were in keys that required the fewest black keys on the piano. I had learned my scales, but I always found it harder to read pieces in keys with a lot of sharps and flats. Whenever I got a new piece, I always looked at the key signature at the beginning to see how many sharps or flats it had, and thus how much trouble I was in. Then I checked on the length.

Miss Perry believed that music should be learned slowly and accurately, and she was right: I found out that if I tried to rip through a new piece and built in a few mistakes, it would take me twice as long to unlearn the mistakes as it would have taken to learn it right the first time. Sometimes, Miss Perry and I disagreed about what "right" was, particularly in the matter of fingering. My music often had little numbers above the notes to indicate that this note should be played by the fourth finger, or that one by the third. Sometimes the fingerings seemed very contorted, especially since I hated crossing my fingers over my thumb. Even though following the suggested fingerings would ultimately have made playing easier and faster, I persisted in concocting my own, and my teachers and I battled about it until I got to college and saw the light.

Every day at home, I practiced for about fifteen or twenty minutes, with my mother never far away; she was always ready to listen to my piece when I was finished working. The piano sat in the living room next to french windows that opened onto the garden. During the spring and the summer, that garden was a terrible distraction, and if my mother hadn't insisted, I probably would have been outside long before those twenty minutes were up. Oddly enough, I didn't learn the lesson of distracting piano placement, and sitting at the keyboard of the instrument in my Boston apartment used to give me a terrific view of the Charles River before I got wise. Now the piano faces a wall.

After a few years, I realized that I had perfect pitch and a good ear, and I could duplicate music I had heard only once at the keyboard. I figured out how to use that gift to make my life easier. Every time my teacher gave me a new piece, she played it through for me once, to give me an idea of the sound of it and to inspire me. This was always at the end of the lesson, ideal for my purposes. After she finished, I would beg, "Oh, Miss Perry, that was so beautiful. Would you just play it for me once more?" Sometimes I'd even flatter her into two repetitions. Then with the rhythm and phrasing from her playing firmly in my head, I would rush home and pick it out on the piano.

This is a useful skill, and it came in handy later, when I played popular music at parties and political rallies (I could pick out the melody of a song if someone sang it to me, and I would add a standard harmony with my left hand). It is also a dangerous crutch, because as a result, I never learned to sight-read very well—to look at a piece of music and figure out what it is supposed to sound like from what the notes look like on the page rather than from the sound of someone else's performance in my ear. Miss Perry caught on after a while and stopped playing my new pieces for me, but the habit remained. Even today, when I have to learn a new piece, I get a recording and listen to it first.

Every spring and fall, Miss Perry's pupils gave recitals. For the children who were natural hams and loved being the center of attention, recitals were bliss; for me, they were terror. As the day crept closer, I felt my hands get clammy and my mouth go dry in anticipation. I was sure I would stumble over the notes in my piece, that I would forget it entirely (it was supposed to be memorized), but there was no escape. Inexorably, the day—always a Sunday afternoon— arrived. Five or six of Miss Perry's pupils, all at about the same level, would assemble in her living room in their best church attire, which for me meant a full-skirted dress, short white socks, and patent leather shoes. Parents, relatives, and neighbors made up the audience.

The least accomplished child played first. At my first recital, when I was five, I was first; eventually I worked my way to the end, as the best of the six-year-olds. Then I moved up a group to be the youngest of the seven-and-eight-year-old set. Playing first was all right—at least you got it over with. Playing last meant an agonizing hour of figurative nail-biting (real nail-biting wasn't allowed) as you awaited your turn, twisting your music in your damp hands, deaf to whatever your friends were doing at the piano. Then came the sinking feeling that it was your turn, and only your hard-learned piano etiquette got you up there. First came the condemned man's walk to the piano, where you sat on the stool, adjusted yourself, got your hands centered, and placed your right foot on the right pedal, left foot on the left pedal. Then came a deep breath, and The Performance, as you prayed all along that you weren't about to make a mistake. Then in a daze you would stand, bow, and try to get back to your seat without tripping over your feet.

It never got any easier—the more I knew, the more potential mistakes there were to be made. In all the years that I played recitals, I only enjoyed my performances afterward. Some of the other children seemed to like it much more: my cousin John Heiss—who later took up the flute and clarinet as well, and who is now a composer on the faculty at the New England Conservatory of Music and the head of its contemporary music group—was also one of those child recitalists, and I don't remember him always wanting to sink into the floor.

That isn't to say that I didn't enjoy performing at all. Private, impromptu playing was delightful. When we visited friends or relatives, or when people came to our house, I was usually called upon to play my party pieces (those brief ones I had memorized), and that was fine. I also remember playing for the sick grandmother of a friend when I was about eight, and knowing that my playing made her happy. Public recitals were an ordeal, a test; with the impromptu performances, I had the sense that I was giving people pleasure, just as I took pleasure in playing for myself, and I could relax. I could never have been a professional musician—I like the sharing, private sort of music-making best. In the early nineteenth century, friends of the composer Franz Schubert used to have parties, called Schubertiades, at which they would get together and play Schubert's chamber music and sing his songs in somebody's living room, and then everybody would dance while Schubert, who hated dancing, played his waltzes on the piano. That's my idea of fun.

During my first few years of piano lessons, all my friends were playing too. I was quite serious about my music, and I made good progress: pretty soon my mother didn't have to be in the next room to be sure I was practicing. But once the teenage years hit, our ranks began to dwindle. Suddenly, current popular songs interrupted my single-minded concentration on classical repertoire. My sister Candy, two years younger than I, stopped her lessons after a few years, but my mother wanted me to go on. When I was twelve, she sensed that I was beginning to lose interest, and she found me a different kind of teacher.

Nancy Fletcher Janssen, my cousin, was pretty, popular, and in her early twenties. She had just graduated from Wellesley and was starting out as a piano teacher. I adored and admired her. My mother thought that if Nancy taught me popular as well as classical music, my interest would remain strong, so Nancy and I split our lessons between Robert Schumann (1810–56), Domenico Scarlatti (1685–1757), on the classical side, and the popular George Gershwin (1898–1937), and Richard Rodgers (1902–79).

Suddenly, learning to play the piano had a more direct relation to the rest of my life. My first popular piece was

Gershwin's "Embraceable You," and when I was twelve I played it on a radio station, WVET in Rochester, that my father had bought with a couple of other World War II veterans. My father took me to *South Pacific;* when I heard the velvety, operatic voice of Ezio Pinza booming into the theater and wooing Mary Martin with "Some Enchanted Evening," I was hooked, and I learned that song along with "Bali Ha'i" and "I'm in Love with a Wonderful Guy." I picked up my mother's Porter favorites, like "You're the Top" and "Night and Day." Romance engulfed me—I swooned over "Smoke Gets in Your Eyes" (I adored Nat King Cole, who sang it in such a sensuous way) and "If I Loved You" from *Carousel.* I was delighted to practice the piano for an hour at a time, several days a week.

Popular music also did great things for my social life. I was shy and gawky ("a late bloomer," my mother always assured me), and at thirteen I had already reached my full height of five feet eight inches. Needless to say, all the boys were much shorter, and boy-girl parties, while irresistible, were a social agony for me. But once I could play popular music, I stayed glued to the piano bench, playing Richard Rodgers' "Lover," "September Song" by Kurt Weill (1900–50), and songs from *Oklahoma!* and *The King and I* for everyone to sing. If there was a song I didn't know, someone would sing the melody for me and I could pick it up right away. All those scales I had played came in handy. Even though I had never studied chords, as guitarists do, I knew instinctively what notes accompanied the melody, and I could improvise on the spot. No longer a wallflower, I was part of the party—and I didn't have to dance with all those short boys.

My mother's idea paid off: my interest in the classical repertoire was renewed. I learned movements from sonatas by Ludwig van Beethoven (1770–1827). I threw myself into one of the lovely *Songs Without Words* by Felix Mendelssohn (1809–47), which had an exquisite accompaniment, like water rippling, in the left hand; the fiery rhythms of a Brahms *Hungarian Dance;* a little finger-bending Franz Liszt (1811–86); a few wonderful Chopin preludes; some sparely elegant Mozart sonatas. I also enjoyed playing arrangements of music from operas: there was the mysterious, insinuating "Barcarole" from *Tales of Hoffman* by Jacques Offenbach (1819–80) and the anguished quartet from *Rigoletto* by Giuseppe Verdi (1813–1901)—Italian drama at its zenith.

Nancy didn't let me learn by ear, and most of these pieces were too complicated to allow it anyway, so I developed a method for learning that I still use. I work on a new piece at the beginning of a practice session, when I'm fresh. I don't do the most tempting thing, which is to play through the piece to the end. Instead, I take a few measures and learn the left-hand part, because otherwise I know I'll give it short shrift, since the right hand usually has the melody. Once I've got it down, I learn the right hand. Once that section is worked out, I go on to some other piece for half an hour—something I'm trying to memorize—or I rework something I learned earlier.

Recitals still went on, no longer in a living room but on stages in a local women's club or the high school auditorium. Now things were even more formal, and there was a much greater distance between me and the audience. I didn't like it any more than before, but I got better at it—the head-up walk to the piano, the gracious bow at the end, the obliviousness to my clammy hands in the middle. Later, when I had to make speeches along with people who'd been in politics all their lives, that early training came in handy.

The social instincts that emerged when I was a teenager created new musical urges for me. Piano playing is a pretty solitary activity unless you are involved in chamber music, and neither I nor my classmates knew anything about that. So when I was in seventh grade, I took up the violin solely to be able to play in the school orchestra. The Bronxville public schools were progressive (miraculously, I was allowed to remain left-handed; nuns in a parochial school would doubtless have forced me into right-handedness) and interested in the arts, so there were plenty of instrumental and choral groups and theatrical productions.

I had become a decent pianist, but I was a terrible violinist. I never practiced at home, just at rehearsals, but pretty soon I was in the orchestra, seated at the very back, of course: orchestral string sections are arranged so the strongest players, who lead the five sections (first violin, second violin, viola, cello, and double bass), are seated at the front of the sections, and the weaker ones are in back. I was also on the inside, because my bowing was never quite in synch. Orchestras have set bowings to make a uniform appearance. Everyone in the section is supposed to draw the bow across the string in the same direction—either from the top of the bow to the bottom or vice versa—on any given note. I was almost always doing the opposite of what everyone else was, so my place was away from the edge of the stage, shielded by the violinist sharing my music stand. I never got thrown out of the orchestra, though. After all those years of exposed recital playing, it was glorious to be so protected. There was none of the pressure that went with climbing up onstage by yourself, and a wrong note was instantly drowned out by the noise of thirty or forty other players.

We gave symphonic concerts, but the playing I enjoyed most was in the pit orchestra for our annual Gilbert and Sullivan operettas. Theater was in my blood. My father was an avid amateur actor, and his idea of relaxation was to perform with the local Bronxville theater group, or the Westchester County Players. He often had leading roles, and this normally shy man caught fire when he was inhabiting a character. I remember him as Thomas à Becket in T. S. Eliot's *Murder in the Cathedral* when I was about ten. The group took over the local Episcopal church for theater in the round on the high altar, up and down the aisles, and behind the audience, with music and candlelight. When he wasn't performing, he took us to every Broadway musical that came out, and he was even coproducer of *Man of La Mancha* in 1965.

Safe in the orchestra pit, I was in on the happy chaos of rehearsals for *The Mikado, H.M.S. Pinafore,* and *The Pirates of Penzance.* The drama teacher yelled at the kids onstage for messing up their lines and the kids backstage for bringing down the curtain at the wrong time, while the conductor yelled at us for coming in wrong. After an absolutely lunatic Tuesday night dress rehearsal, they would always groan, "This show needs two more weeks," but somehow, on Friday, the curtain would go up, and we'd all do what we were supposed to. With the little light on my music stand, I could focus on the music in the darkness, but I could look ahead and see the conductor, look out into the house and see the audience, and crane my neck to see the actors up onstage. It was the best place to be.

In senior high school, I moved out of the orchestra and onto the stage. If I was a good pianist and a less good violinist, I was a much worse singer. Still, I could carry a tune and read music, making me a great catch for the second soprano section, which always had the harmony parts. (First sopranos sang the melody, which was easier.) We'd sweep around the stage in long dresses and sigh "Twenty lovesick maidens we" from *Patience.* I even got a small solo part once as a page boy in *Ruddigore,* and I went onstage all decked out in tights and a tunic, my long hair tucked up under a cap.

By the end of high school, I was still pretty serious, going home to my books and my piano while my friends were chasing boys or vice versa. Music remained my best means of expression, but it was mostly private pleasure. It never occurred to me to consider being a professional musician: it wasn't that I was untalented, and I certainly worked hard, but for me, performance was never a calling, and it has to be if you're going to triumph over all the difficulties a performing career involves. I didn't want to practice for hours every day, either, or enter competitions, learn vast amounts of repertoire, or throw myself into the incredibly competitive world of concert artists. I planned to continue to study music in college, but it would be for my own enjoyment.

TWO

College and Opera

IN THE MID-1950s, most of the best colleges were single-sex institutions. Because I wanted to go to a Catholic college, I decided on Manhattanville, which was just a forty-five-minute drive north of New York City in Westchester County. Three of my Bronxville friends joined me there.

Manhattanville, formerly in Manhattan, had moved up to Westchester just a few years earlier. It was a pretty, verdant, fifteen-acre campus, built on an estate that had belonged to Whitelaw Reid, owner of the *Herald Tribune*. The college was operated by the nuns of the Sacred Heart, a highly educated order founded in France in 1800. I majored in English, so that I could read as many novels as I liked, but I also wanted to continue my piano lessons, so I took a minor in music.

College was primarily a social time for me: my mother's

predictions about "late blooming" came true, and I passed from the shy, gawky stage into having many boyfriends, so many that the campus joke was that I would surprise everyone and become a nun. I did manage to get an education, however, and the musical advantages of Manhattanville turned out to be great. For the first time, I became quite interested in Catholic liturgical music, what with daily mass and high mass on Sundays. (High mass was an hour long instead of a half hour, and the extra time was mostly devoted to music.)

Mass was held in the college chapel in Manhattanville's main building. Whitelaw Reid had built himself a stone Italian castle, which was vast, baronial, and ornate. The students called it "the Castle," and it housed the administrative offices and the nuns' quarters. The former library, with its vaulted ceiling, stained glass windows, and parquet floors, had become the chapel.

Daily mass had no choir, only the ten most devout girls and ten nuns who sat in front and led everyone else, but on Sundays, the forty-member choir sang Kyries and Glorias from masses by great church composers. The wonderful organ pealed out Bach preludes or murmured quietly during the meditative moments. The service was sung entirely in Latin, and it was mystical and wonderful. I never felt quite the same about going to mass after the Second Vatican Council in 1962–65, when the liturgy went from Latin to the vernacular. For one thing, the music was never as good again.

The Manhattanville campus at the time was also home to the Pius X School of Liturgical Music, a center where priests and nuns would come from all over the country to train in sacred music, and then go back to their seminaries to teach it. The school was housed in our music building, so when I went there to practice the piano, I would hear Gregorian chant wafting through the halls. I loved the otherworldliness of chant: its unembellished, single line was direct, serious, and open-ended, and without harmony or predictable rhythm it seemed such a contrast to the much more elaborate, balanced Mozart or Chopin that I was playing. Chant *felt* medieval; it conjured up an air of mystery—of vaulted cathedrals and monasteries, and early centuries of faith. Vatican II pretty much did away with chant, which is a shame, because it is such a profoundly spiritual music.

Mother Morgan was the head of Manhattanville's music department. My piano teachers were all laypeople who also taught in New York City at Juilliard and the Manhattan School of Music. Nuns at Manhattanville mostly taught philosophy, theology, and English, but Mother Morgan was an exception, and she was a powerful figure. She was very popular, probably because of her infectious zest for music and living. I was in the hundred-voice concert choir (in the second soprano section, as usual), which mixed sacred and secular music and gave four big concerts a year. Mother Morgan was our conductor. Like all the nuns, she was always in full habit, and she conducted with grand, sweeping gestures, her long sleeves flying about, as she emoted to the ecstatic "Hallelujah Chorus" from *Messiah* by George Frideric Handel (1685–1759).

The Sacred Heart nuns were cloistered and therefore not allowed to leave the Manhattanville campus. I think Mother Morgan had more fun than most of them, because her music connected her to the outside world. Musicians came up from New York to give concerts, and she would meet and look after them and sit through their performances rapt and delighted. Mother Morgan thought that music was fun. As part of the mass, it was practical; in concert it was an overflowing expression of joy, or sorrow, or celebration. For her, music was a robust, integral part of life, and that spirit rubbed off on all of us.

The Manhattanville students were not cloistered, of course. Our weekends meant treks to Yale and other men's colleges in pursuit of amusement and that all-consuming "MRS degree," but the school also offered us more serious opportunities for escape. Several evenings a week, a dozen or so tickets were available for the Metropolitan Opera, and the first girls to sign up boarded a bus for the city. For my first two years at Manhattanville, I was always among them.

We sat at the very top of the old Met, right under the ceiling, at the score desks with their little reading lights. We were supposed to be following the scores of the operas, and we did some of that, but we also did a fair amount of flirting with the boys from Juilliard and Columbia, graduate students who were also supposed to be studying. It was a treasure trove of older men—they must have been in their twenties.

They were serious music lovers and devoted followers of the operatic scene. They followed music the way sports fans follow baseball teams—a new singer was cause for tremendous excitement, while the cancellation by a favorite meant a combination of groans of dismay and anticipation about who would replace him or her.

I had a concentrated dose of opera in those two years, and I discovered that it was full-scale, full-blown entertainment. My evenings at the Met banished forever the idea that opera is just long stretches of serious music in incomprehensible languages. Opera was show biz, just like those Broadway shows my father was always taking me to. There were costumes and scenery. There were exotic settings, like Egypt in Verdi's *Aida,* which has that wonderful Triumphal March with blaring trumpets. Murder and mayhem were at the heart of operas like Verdi's *Rigoletto,* in which a court jester tries to assassinate the lustful duke who abducts his daughter Gilda, but ends up killing Gilda instead. (The final act features the famous quartet that I played in a piano arrangement.)

I always cried through the death of the little seamstress Mimi at the end of *La Bohème,* the Giacomo Puccini (1858–1924) story of a group of poor artists in Paris. It's a notorious tearjerker, as is the end of Puccini's *Madama Butterfly* when the Japanese "wife" of an American naval officer gives up their child to him and commits suicide when he returns to Japan, after several years' absence, with his "real" American wife. Puccini excelled in portraying frail but loving women who come to pathetic ends. The sopranos who sing the parts, however, have to have extremely robust voices in order to cut through his thick orchestrations.

To get past the language problem, I read the texts (librettos) of the operas in advance. Some of those librettos don't make a lot of sense, but once the music gets going, it doesn't matter. The plot of Mozart's *Don Giovanni,* for instance, gets stranger and stranger. In the end, the statue of a man whom the Don has murdered comes to his house for dinner and drags the famous seducer off to hell. That statue has one of the best vocal parts in the opera: his low, threatening bass voice pounds out its message ("Repent!") above roiling arpeggio figures in the orchestra that grow in intensity to a stupendous climax.

I was inundated with Italian and German opera. There was a wonderful production of *The Barber of Seville* by Gioacchino Rossini (1792–1868), which is a madcap romp—its overture gets faster and faster until you think the wind players must run out of breath and collapse, setting the tone for what is to follow. The high-spirited heroine, Rosina, was played by Roberta Peters, an American soprano then in her early twenties, who had just made her Met debut a few years earlier. She had never sung on an opera stage before she was called in to replace an indisposed singer at the last moment, and she soon became the darling of the Met.

Rosina shows up in a Mozart opera too: in 1786, thirty years before Rossini wrote *Barber,* Mozart used the same source, plays by the French writer Beaumarchais, to tell the second chapter of Rosina's story in his wonderful opera *The Marriage of Figaro.* In this opera she is married to the Count she went to such trouble to get in *Barber,* but now he's a philanderer, chasing after Susanna, who's about to marry Figaro, the barber. In *Barber,* Rosina is a feisty young girl with lots of fast, ornamented singing (coloratura); in *Figaro,* she's the tragic, wronged countess, and an entirely different kind of singer, a dramatic soprano, with two beautiful, slow arias. I saw the wonderful, handsome baritone George London sing the role of the Count; years later, I met him at a party in Washington. Meeting opera singers is great fun: they're always a bit larger than life.

The Met was full of exciting singers in those years. There was the tenor Richard Tucker, who looked so funny as the romantic lead (he was short and tubby), but he sang thrillingly. Risë Stevens was sultry and beautiful as Carmen, the fateful gypsy. I've always loved *Carmen.* Even though Georges Bizet (1838–75) was French, his music conjures up the hot passions of Spain, and the quick and dirty story makes it a great introductory opera. I saw lots of Richard Wagner (1813–83) too, including *Tristan und Isolde* and *Lohengrin.* My friends used to tease me about how much I loved Wagner, especially considering I don't really like the sound of the German language. They thought those operas were incredibly long and boring, and the Wagnerian singers, who had the biggest voices, were invariably the fattest and most incongruous-looking. I didn't care what it looked like or how long it was: I'd close my eyes and let the wonderfully lush sound of Wagner's huge orchestra envelop me.

Wagnerians aren't necessarily fat anymore: the whole attitude toward opera staging has changed, and singers are supposed to look as well as sound the part. Now when I go to those operas, the singers project character through acting as well as those huge voices, and you can follow the stories, which are full of excitement and romance. A comic book company has even put out a comic book version of Wagner's four-opera saga of gods, heroes, and villains, *The Ring of the Nibelung,* which is just as action-packed as any superhero story.

People associate opera with foreign singers, and certainly there are many, such as the great tenors Luciano Pavarotti and Plácido Domingo, who are even media stars today. But American singers started to break through during World War II, when the European singers were trapped in their war-torn countries, and in the days when I was first going to the Met, there were plenty of American stars—Richard Tucker, Roberta Peters, Robert Merrill (a baritone who reminded me of Ezio Pinza, whom I'd heard in *South Pacific*), and Jan Peerce, who, like Tucker, had been a synagogue cantor. (Years later, Peerce and I were fellow performers in a political benefit concert.) The Americans were a special treat in Mozart's *The Magic Flute,* which the Met did in English. *The Magic Flute* was written for the eighteenth-century Viennese equivalent of Broadway, far from the courts of the nobility (Mozart's usual hangout). As a result, it has dialogue and amusing low-life characters, like the bird catcher Papageno who can't do anything right but ends up with a wife anyway. It was a big switch to hear the opera in English and be able to laugh at all the jokes.

I found out why I called people who always had to have their own way "prima donnas"—it means "first lady" in

Italian and refers to the leading soprano part in the opera (the subordinate woman's role is the "second donna"). The prima donna gets the star dressing room, and everyone caters to her. If she has a cold, or doesn't like her costume, or thinks that someone is trying to upstage her, watch out. Tenors, the high-voiced men who usually sing the romantic leads, have similar characteristics. You have to sympathize: singers, unlike instrumental musicians—who have violins or cellos that, however beloved, are replaceable—have to depend on the little vocal cords in their throats for their livelihood, and it makes them a bit paranoid. Singing is also hard physical labor, so ailments are as incapacitating as they are for any athlete. A high-strung performer also often makes for a more electrifying performance—the great soprano Maria Callas was famous for that—and stories about "temperament" are half the fun for the opera fan, who follows them as the film buff does the marriages and divorces of movie stars.

On off days from college, I was also launching my own little performing career, which had absolutely nothing to do with classical music. Television was in its infancy, and I started doing some commercial acting. All dressed up, trotting around New York to auditions and go-sees with my portfolio, I got a taste of show-biz frustration, but I also landed a few jobs. I was the Revlon Hairspray girl for a while on "The $64,000 Question" before it exploded in scandal. I was also one of the gang on "Coke Time with Eddie Fisher" a fifteen-minute show. He sang, and during the two or three commercial breaks, a few of us would drink Coke for the camera in our bobby socks, saddle shoes, and poodle skirts. I was supposed to do a Coke-drinking bit with the great Eddie himself, but he had a tantrum when he realized I was a foot taller than he was, and he'd have to stand on a box next to me. Drinking Coke for a national audience isn't exactly singing at the Met, but it had its challenges. The piece of direction I'll always remember is the stern admonition "Don't you burp, young lady!"

It was my first experience of being around the stagestruck: teenagers constantly mobbed Fisher and his wife, Debbie Reynolds, backstage. Little did I know I'd turn into a mad groupie myself in later years. Also, sometimes in later years, when I was standing under TV lights with a microphone stuck under my nose and a reporter throwing a question at me and waiting for me to trip up, I'd think, I've done live TV before. This is nothing.

One of my other gigs was singing with Perry Como on TV. Just a few years ago, I attended a Perry Como concert on the Cape and went backstage afterward to see him. We hadn't met since those days, and it was as though the intervening thirty-odd years had never been when Como looked hard at me and exclaimed, "Joan Bennett! What have you been doing all these years?"

In between dates, acting, and trips to the opera, I did manage to get some practicing done, and in May 1958, it was time for my senior recital, a graduation requirement for music majors and minors. It was probably the longest and most exposed performing I'd done: there was no one else on the program, and I had to play forty-five minutes of music that would demonstrate my mastery of what I'd been working on during my four years. Somehow, though, it didn't create that sinking feeling in the pit of my stomach that all those recitals of my elementary and high school years had.

The audience was certainly more knowledgeable: here were the piano faculty, the music students, and all my friends and roommates. But it was just me: no competition with anyone coming before or after, and no sense that the audience was sitting in judgment on me. It was a requirement, and it was unlikely that I would fail, unless I really made a mess. For the girls who were planning to go on in music and become teachers, the stakes were certainly higher. But for me, it was expected only that I would do my best and get my grade—what it was didn't much matter—and that would be that.

The idea was to demonstrate that I had mastered the range of the piano literature. I built my program chronologically, as was the custom; I suppose the assumption was that you listened to music as the people at the time would have heard it. People listening to Bach (1685–1750) would not have heard Mozart (1756–91), for example. So I started off with some of my favorite Bach, crisp, efficient, and mind-stretching as ever, and went on to some witty, ebullient Haydn (1732–1809). Next came a Mozart sonata, the longest piece on the program, which in its three movements (fast-slow-fast) encapsulated the elegance and undercurrents of passion that Mozart always means to me. Next came the nineteenth century, and a move into more heart-on-the-sleeve Romanticism with some short pieces: some of the fleet *Papillons* (Butterflies) by Robert Schumann (1810–56), a Chopin (1810–49) waltz or two, and some exquisite Brahms (1833–97) *Intermezzi*.

I finished up with a Debussy *Arabesque*. The Impressionism of Claude Debussy (1862–1918), delicate and subtly colored like Monet's water lily paintings, was about as modern as I got; I never played any of the twentieth-century greats, such as Béla Bartók (1881–1945). Things have changed, and now twentieth-century music is a staple from the earliest years of piano training. I loved those Debussy *Arabesques,* though. I still keep them warmed up and ready, so that if I'm asked to play a benefit, I can whip one out and play it back to back with Debussy's funny, syncopated *Golli-*

wogg's Cake-walk. It's hard to believe that the two are by the same composer, because the *Arabesque* is so dreamy and pretty, and the *Cake-walk,* as the title implies, is ragtime. It makes a great show, brief and satisfying.

For that last Manhattanville recital, I once again donned my best dress and shoes and walked out onstage, this time in the music department's auditorium, which was big enough to hold the whole school of about sixteen hundred students and faculty. I made it through my program respectably, without any major disasters—no slips of the fingers, no lapses of memory. I felt professional. And as my friends gathered around me afterward to offer their congratulations when I had finished, I felt a tremendous relief. I was *not* a professional. I would never have to do this again. I was going to get married, I would play for my children and for myself, and music once again would become something private, without pressure.

I had no idea that this was only the beginning of my life as a performer. Marriage into the Kennedy family meant total immersion in politics, and in politics everybody pulls his or her weight. My talent was for music, so that's what I was soon called upon to do.

THREE

Politics

MY SENIOR YEAR of college went as you might expect for a shy, sheltered girl studying piano and reading novels under the watchful guidance of a campus full of Catholic nuns. I spent the entire spring in a series of tiny, soundproofed practice rooms (with a window if I was lucky; usually not) rather like nuns' cells, getting ready for that senior recital, concentrating on a series of pieces to be mastered absolutely. But the seeds of change had already been sowed in that quiet, well-ordered existence. That year, when the Kennedy family descended on Manhattanville to dedicate a building, Jean Smith introduced me to her brother Ted, youngest of the Kennedy sons, and still unmarried.

I was to go abruptly from a private, eminently predictable life of contemplation in a windowless cubicle to the rough-and-tumble arena of national politics. Two years after I graduated, I was politicking like mad for John F. Kennedy in the mines of West Virginia. Piano playing was put on hold for a while. The study of music, after all, is in some ways the absolute opposite of politics—the great politician thrives on knowing something about everything, while conservatory life demands hermetic, single-minded devotion. But curiously enough, music eventually proved useful to the family business.

Ted and I were married, after a three-month engagement, on Thanksgiving 1958, when Ted had a week off from law school. During the months between my graduation and my marriage, I lived with my parents in Bronxville and saw very little of Ted, because when he wasn't at school in Virginia, he was up in Massachusetts managing his brother Jack's Senate reelection campaign. Once we were engaged, I spent the occasional weekend in Massachusetts tagging along with Ted, his sister Eunice, and Jack as they campaigned in old factory and fishing towns like Fall River and New Bedford.

That was my introduction to politics, the basic grass-roots, press-the-flesh kind. There would be coffee parties in the mornings at the homes of supporters, a Rotary club lunch, a visit to a factory and an interview at a radio station in the afternoon, a rally in the evening. I remember it as a whirl as we rushed from one event to the next (there was never enough time to see everyone) and an endless meal (we were always eating, whatever we were offered or could snatch up along the way, because we never knew when we'd have another chance). It was exciting and a real look into Ted's life for me. Still, I felt rather like a tourist—entertained, but as though none of what was going on really had anything to do with me. After all, there had never been any talk of Ted going into politics himself. He was still planning on private practice after his graduation from law school.

I suppose that was a fairly naive assumption. That Senate

campaign was no one-shot deal—I had married into politics, and once you're in office, you're campaigning all the time. By the following summer, the Kennedys were sitting around in my father-in-law's Hyannis Port house talking about running Jack in the 1960 Democratic presidential primaries. There were no professional campaigners in those days—your relatives and your college roommates did the job—so Ted was appointed coordinator for the Rocky Mountain states, and that fall, Ted and I went west "hunting delegates." Our job was to sound people out about Jack, whom few of them had heard of. Most people were backing Lyndon Johnson, and Hubert Humphrey, Stuart Symington, and Henry "Scoop" Jackson were also in the running. We had to persuade them to keep open minds.

It couldn't have been less glamorous, but it was certainly a way to see the country. I remember spending one entire week in a car (I was six months pregnant at the time), rattling over the western slopes of the Rockies. It was just Ted and me and our driver, a young lawyer out of Denver named "Whizzer" White, a.k.a. Byron White, then a former All-American football player and Rhodes scholar, today a justice of the Supreme Court. That trip included Aspen, Colorado, which had unpaved, muddy streets and looked more like 1859 than 1959, a far cry from the posh resort it is today.

When our daughter Kara was born in February, Ted was in Wisconsin, a key primary state, since by then Jack was a declared candidate and the heat was on. I got about six weeks of straight motherhood, and then I was off on the road as well, leaving Kara with a nanny in Washington, where we had moved to be with the rest of the family. My first primary state was West Virginia, important because it was only one percent Catholic, and if Jack could win there, or do well, it would augur well for a national race.

Sometimes I was out campaigning with Ted, or with my

mother-in-law Rose (the best in the family), or with Jack. I was with Jack a lot, since Jackie Kennedy was pregnant and couldn't travel. I was learning the ropes, and my job was to look nice and be friendly. I looked so nice and friendly that when I went down into those West Virginia mines with Jack, I got whistled at by the miners. Those were the days when getting whistled at was considered a compliment, and the political managers around Jack thought that I was doing just fine. It turned into a bit of a joke: when Jack's campaign people sat around talking about "Where can we use the mother?" or "Where do we pull the sister in?" and my name came up, invariably someone would answer with "Joan? She's too beautiful to use." Jack thought it was great, and when he gave everybody souvenirs at the end of the campaign, mine was a cigarette box with those words engraved on it.

I got to use my national campaign training very soon. With Jack elected President, Ted's father thought it would be a good idea to keep Jack's Senate seat in the family. Ted was the obvious choice, so all thoughts of private practice were put on hold—permanently, as it turned out. In November 1960, Ted and I moved to Boston to start preparing for the 1962 Senate race. This time, we were on our own. Everybody else was down in Washington running the country, so Ted and I started the grass-roots round ourselves. I wasn't watching anymore, I was doing, and being able to play the piano came in very handy.

Now, at those morning coffees and afternoon teas in suburban houses, after we'd shaken hands with everyone, and Ted had given a little pep talk, I would be asked to play the piano. I'd get the hostess to tell me what her favorite songs were—they often turned out to be some of those show tunes that came in handy at parties when I was a teenager—and, if

I was lucky, everyone would sing along. Sometimes I'd play a classical piece, something short, pleasant, and unobtrusive, like a Chopin waltz or two, so that people could keep on talking if they wanted to. The object, after all, was not music but politics.

My playing was a diversion, something to do during the time we were there, and people enjoyed it. They thought it was nice that I had a "talent" to share, and it was certainly an icebreaker. After I played, someone always came over to tell me about her little daughter who played the piano, and how she hoped someday her daughter would play as well as I did. People appreciated seeing the candidate's wife contribute something, and it was a way for them to get to know something about me.

I never thought of those times as "performing." It was more relaxed than that, with a communal feeling, like the afternoons back in Bronxville when I was a kid and my parents would announce that little Joan would play her latest piece for the relatives. Even at the bigger rallies, held in halls rather than living rooms, it was not a concert. I'd do my Chopin, and then if I was lucky, someone would say, "Let's sing," and everyone would roar out "Hey, Look Me Over" (that was Ted's campaign theme, a march with a good beat) or some patriotic song, or, if Rose was on the program, "Sweet Adeline," which had been her father's favorite song. Irish songs were a big deal in Kennedy campaigns. (I've had to brush them up recently now that my son Patrick is carrying on the family tradition.) I also learned a lot of other national songs: Italian ones for Boston's North End neighborhoods, Greek ones for some of the other suburbs.

Playing the piano was a lot easier than speaking was for me. Speaking was also part of my role, and it took me a long time to get comfortable doing it. I didn't have to give big speeches—I'd get up and thank whoever organized the event and Ted's supporters, and I'd encourage them to get out and vote for my husband. Sometimes I was on my own, playing the smaller towns, while Ted hit the big towns and the cities. It reminds me a bit of the way the music world works. The young, less experienced violinist or pianist performs in smaller towns, in smaller halls, and with less celebrated orchestras, learning the ropes and the repertoire, while the more famous artist, who can draw a crowd, plays the bigger halls and solos with the prestigious orchestras.

Those little towns are a wonderful opportunity for the young performer, and they were great for me. You feel as though your audience really wants you. Getting up in front of a big crowd in an important hall brings its own rush of excitement, but playing or speaking for a small group, when you can see the face of every person in the audience, has a much more personal feeling. You feel as though they'll forgive you your mistakes, that they don't mind your using them to learn, as long as you're giving it your best effort.

Unlike the young artist, who plays the small towns to get experience for the big ones, the candidate's wife doesn't usually move on to the big time on her own. But I did. Ted spent the entire 1964 Senate campaign in the hospital recovering from a plane crash that broke his back, so I had to represent him all over the state. By then we had two children, but we had a good nanny in Boston, and I was able to engineer my traveling so I'd never have to be away more than two days at a time. Still, I was on the road six days a week. I'd hit a VFW hall in Springfield and relay Ted's greeting from his hospital bed, asking his supporters to keep up the good work. Then I'd read his speech. There wasn't much occasion for piano playing on that campaign, but I had a great time. Speaking was easier as I got used to it—after all, no one expected me to really deliver the speech the way Ted would have, though I did my best to give it some spin.

I got my usual role back in later campaigns. In 1968, for example, when Bobby Kennedy was running in the Democratic presidential primaries, I got to be substitute consort again—this time, Ethel was pregnant and not traveling. Bobby's theme was that wonderful Woody Guthrie tune, "This Land Is Your Land," and whenever we were somewhere with a piano, I played it. Now, everybody knew that music was what I loved—after all, I had been the President's sister-in-law, and all the Kennedys had been dissected in the media. I had also started narrating with orchestra, and people had seen me do *Peter and the Wolf* with the Boston Pops on national television. So when we were on the road, Ethel got asked about her many children, and I was asked about music—even though, for me, music and children went together.

FOUR

Narrating and Music-Making in Washington

WASHINGTON TODAY has a lively mix of cultural institutions, but when Ted and I arrived there in 1962 as the newly minted Massachusetts senator and wife, it was far from a musical town. Jackie Kennedy displayed the White House's interest in classical music when she invited the great Spanish cellist Pablo Casals to perform there, but apart from such occasional special concerts, there were only a few regular opportunities to hear live music. The National Symphony, then a small-time operation without the stature and history of the great orchestras of Boston, New York, Cleveland, Chicago, and Philadelphia, was the main event.

The orchestra's board members were delighted to have a young senator's wife with an interest in music join them. It was my first in-depth look at what an orchestra does, how it works, and who pays for it. But I was soon to get the performer's-eye view of it as well. Since I had young children, it seemed natural for me to be involved in children's musical activities, and in 1965 I was asked to narrate *Peter and the Wolf.*

There are several very popular orchestral works which include narration. Most, like *Peter and the Wolf* by the Russian composer Sergei Prokofiev (1891–1953), are aimed at children. *Peter* is charming: the story, about a little boy, his grandfather, and various animals, is an introduction to the orchestra, but the absorbing story and the delightful music make it much more than a pedagogical exercise. The narrator tells the story, and the characters and events are graphically represented in the music. Peter, whose sprightly, carefree theme is carried by the violins, is clearly both resourceful and mischievous. The grandfather is a gruff bassoon, his music slow and deliberate, and the hapless duck a mournful, nasal oboe line that evokes the waddling creature to perfection. The duck has a musical argument with the bird, represented by the trilling flute, and when the wolf, represented by a frightening rumble of three horns, chases the cat, a sinuous clarinet, up the tree, we hear the clarinet go in a quick upward scale.

Narration pieces are usually programmed on pops concerts—orchestral concerts that feature arrangements of show tunes and lighter classical works, like Strauss waltzes. They are also favorites for benefit concerts, because orchestras can bring in a celebrity who will attract a crowd beyond the music lovers—an actor, a sports figure, a newscaster, a comedian, or a political figure, like me.

I had an advantage over most narrators in having musical training, but I don't think I'd ever studied so hard for a performance as I did for that first *Peter and the Wolf.* Working with an orchestra is a whole different ball game from playing solo piano. In a solo recital, if you miss a note, or change tempo, or decide to play a passage a little more softly than you did when you rehearsed it, it's no big deal. Try that with an orchestra and you're lost or drowned out, though experienced conductors can almost always rescue you (I have a funny story about that, which I'll tell later). I had never worked as a soloist with an orchestra and conductor before, so I was leaving nothing to chance, and I wound up prepared within an inch of my life.

I assumed I had to learn the whole score, so true to my old habits, I started listening to records. Dozens of people have recorded *Peter and the Wolf.* I listened carefully in order to get my entrances down cold, because they can be complicated in *Peter and the Wolf:* often the music is playing when you start speaking, so you have to know exactly which note you are supposed to start on, and how long you have before you are supposed to finish. Narrators don't speak in strict time with the music, of course—that would be very unnatural— but you have to finish your lines within the musical phrase, or it sounds wrong. I was determined not to have to rely on the conductor for cues as to when to start and when to finish. What if he forgot? So I studied that score for weeks. I would be allowed to read it and follow it during the performance, but by the time of the rehearsal—and I was only going to get one—I barely needed it, because I could probably have sung every instrument's part in the whole piece from memory. Needless to say, I had all my cues down cold. The conductor was in shock.

By the evening of the concert, I was all set. Decked out in my best yellow velvet evening gown with white beading on the shoulders, and with my hair—half mine and half falls and wiglets—all teased sixties-style into a blond tower, I was nervous but determined not to make a fool of myself. The audience was full of my symphony board friends, my husband's colleagues and family (Ethel Kennedy, Eunice

Shriver, and lots of nieces and nephews, all very supportive and proud), and not least, Kara and Teddy, ages five and four.

Narrating turned out to be an incredible thrill. Sure, I had performed before: I'd played my recitals, and I'd given speeches or played short pieces in front of hundreds of people while campaigning (to say nothing of drinking Coke on national television!), but this was something else. I stood at the very front of the stage behind the lectern, and there, behind me, was an eighty-plus member orchestra, its huge, lush sound sweeping out around me and enveloping me. Narrating is a kind of concerto for speaker and orchestra: sometimes I spoke alone, sometimes the orchestra played alone, and sometimes we were together, and it felt as though the orchestra was a huge wave, holding me up. At moments it swept me away dizzyingly and completely, and it was all I could do to keep paying attention and not lose my place while the orchestra unleashed all those decibels behind me. By the time we reached the final triumphant procession of Peter, his friends, the hunters, and the captured wolf with the unfortunate duck quacking away inside its stomach, I was in love.

It looked as though I had found my performing niche, because the next year Arthur Fiedler and the Boston Pops invited me to narrate *Peter* in Boston. After that, I did at least one narration a year in Boston and elsewhere. (In the fall of 1976, during Ted's Senate reelection campaign, I went into high gear and did them all over Massachusetts, sometimes two or three a week.) I worked with Fiedler six times, occasionally on television, as well as with his assistant conductor, Harry Ellis Dickson, doing pops concerts, benefits, and youth concerts.

Fiedler conducted the Pops for nearly fifty years and essentially put the pops genre on the American map. The Boston Pops formula is unabashedly geared toward entertainment: patrons sit at tables on the ground level of the concert hall, where they can order food and drink. The concerts, which have two intermissions to permit more socializing, consist of short overtures, a concerto, often with a young soloist, and finally a big work or a series of show tune arrangements. Pops concerts are very popular with benefit audiences: since I've lived in Boston, I regularly buy up tables and resell them for charity events.

Fiedler himself was a legend. When I knew him, he was a gruff, white-haired old man with a passion for fire engines, and he gave me lots of good advice about narrating. He was always yelling at me, "Keep your head up! Let's see your pretty face, young lady! These people didn't pay good money to see the top of your head!" He was famous for his bad temper too, but we only had one major run-in when, after I had been working with him for a few years, I made a small modification in the *Peter and the Wolf* text. At the end of the piece, the narrator explains how you can still hear the duck quacking away inside the wolf, "because in his haste, he had swallowed her alive." I always found the mental image created by those words a bit grotesque, and possibly frightening to children, so I added, "Without even harming a feather." Fiedler was apoplectic, but I got my way in the end.

As I got more deeply into narrating, I learned more pieces. My favorite is *The Young Person's Guide to the Orchestra* by Benjamin Britten (1913–76). The English composer wrote the piece for an educational film about the instruments of the orchestra, but it has since become very popular in the concert hall. Britten based the work on a majestic theme by the English composer Henry Purcell (c. 1659–95). The score can stand on its own without the narration, which points out the families of instruments as they appear. Britten wrote thirteen variations on Purcell's theme to showcase all the sections. I especially enjoy the playful clarinet variation and the mournful viola aria, which has little flute tweets above it to leaven its basically sad character. The variations get further and further away from the original theme, but at the end, the orchestra gets put back together in a huge fugue, in which all the sections play the theme in turn, with everything tumbling out louder and louder. The piece is a big job for the narrator, because most of the variations are less than a minute long, and the speaker has to keep jumping in with the text, because the music doesn't stop. By the time we get to the fugue, and I have to call out the entering instruments every few measures, I'm going like mad. Sometimes I like to put on a recording of *Young Person's Guide* and relax and listen to the piece without narration or nerves.

I've also done the patriotic *Lincoln Portrait* by Aaron Copland (1900–90)—in which the text is comprised of sections of the Gettysburg Address and other words by Lincoln—and *Journey into Jazz* by Gunther Schuller (1925–). *Journey* was a real challenge for me, because of its syncopations and instrumentation. I usually follow the violins to keep my place in the score when I narrate, because I used to play violin myself, but for this piece, I had to learn to follow brass instruments and the jazz quintet in front of the orchestra. *Journey* is about a teenage boy who discovers jazz and learns to express all that painful adolescent turmoil through his trumpet playing and improvisation. Getting to know the brass was fun— there's a moment when the narrator talks about the "raw and ugly" notes that the young trumpet player comes out with, and you hear them snarled as only the brass can. It's good to remember sometimes that music, like life, is far from all sweetness and light.

Just recently, I started doing *Carnival of the Animals* by Camille Saint-Saëns (1835–1921), probably the simplest narration of all because there's no real coordination required:

the music stops before I speak, and then starts again after I finish. I was dubious about it at first, because the Ogden Nash poems that precede the animal vignettes are so silly, but it turned out to be charming. My favorite parts include "The Swan," a sinuous melody for cello (and a popular recital encore piece), the lumbering elephants waltzing to a double bass theme, and the watery aquarium, with its swooping glockenspiel.

I got to be quite a pro at narrating. In the beginning, conductors tried to influence my "interpretations." They would want me to get very dramatic: to wave my hand to show the bird in the tree in *Peter,* for example, or shrug my shoulders when the grandfather was annoyed. But it never worked. It didn't feel natural to me. So I evolved my own, fairly straight way of narrating, with no actressy frills.

This was just as well, because I usually got just one rehearsal with the orchestra the morning of the concert or the day before—sometimes it was just a twenty-minute run-through. Orchestras usually have three or four rehearsals for a regular symphony program, but the point of pops is to put on a concert that the orchestra can basically sight-read, that is, play with only minimal rehearsal, if any. Orchestras are expensive to run: musicians get paid by the service, which can be either a three-hour-long rehearsal or a concert, so the more services they play, the more the orchestra costs. Pops concerts are a good way to employ musicians and bring in audiences who probably wouldn't be interested in a regular symphony program, but nobody wants to spend a penny more than necessary to do it.

So my twenty-minute rehearsal is really a matter of fine tuning. We all know the piece. What's in question is tempo —how fast it will be played—and any eccentricities that the soloist and the conductor need to find out about each other. For example, often the conductor doesn't realize before we meet that my voice is pretty soft. I use a microphone, but it can only be turned up so high before my voice starts to sound distorted and strident. So at the rehearsal, the conductor figures out how quiet he has to keep the brass section of the orchestra so that I won't be drowned out. Sometimes, the conductor might want me to say a line a little earlier, so I'll make a note in the score.

After all these years, my scores are covered with arrows, underlining, and little notes to myself. (*Peter and the Wolf* is practically unreadable—some words are underlined so heavily for emphasis that I can't even tell what the words are anymore.) I have all sorts of hieroglyphics and cryptic messages. I'll have "Deep breath here" if the passage coming up is a long sentence, or "Look up" (an Arthur Fiedler legacy) when I don't come in for half a page. Someone once told me to look to the farthest person in the last balcony, and I do that, or I focus on someone I know in the audience. Looking up has its dangers, however—if you look up, you lose your place—so I have to remember to keep my finger on the spot where I left off, or better yet, on the spot where I'll begin again.

Professional soloists don't usually use music in concert performance, unless they are performing a contemporary piece that they've just learned. After all, they play these things week in and week out, so they have a chance to have their parts "in their voices" or "in their fingers." Some conductors even work from memory, which I find incredible. How can they remember all the purely mechanical aspects of performing: everybody's part, all the entrances, all the balances and tempos, as well as the interpretive aspects of a piece that may be an hour long? I know my pieces pretty well too by now, but since I only perform once a year or so, I really need that security blanket, whether I've got the piece memorized or not. Using the music has gotten me in trouble, though. Once I was doing *Peter and the Wolf,* and I suddenly lost my concentration and started to read one of my notes to myself instead of my line. It was just the first word, and I caught myself and went on, but it reminded me of how important total concentration is when you're performing, especially live. I've made lots of television and radio public service announcements, and if you mess up in a recording studio, they can always do it over—twenty times if necessary. But when you're performing live, there are no retakes, so you'd better be with it all the time.

One of the best things about narrating was getting to know orchestra musicians. At the Boston Symphony, which has really become my musical home, the players will come over and talk to me. The oboist always throws an arm around my shoulder and says, "Remember me? I'm the duck!"

When I was first narrating, being an orchestra musician was a hard job that didn't pay especially well. Few orchestras played enough concerts to provide a full-time living for their members, so most musicians had to teach or drive cabs to make enough money to support themselves and their families. Things are different now. There are many more orchestras—every small town in the United States seems to have one—and union bargaining has made the orchestra musician's situation better. Many more ensembles now have contracts that last the whole year, instead of a few months, and guarantee their players considerable salaries. Some of the more prestigious orchestras have salaries that start at around sixty thousand dollars and go up from there, with extra payment for overtime and recording. Musicians no longer have to compromise their standard of living in order to do what they love—play an instrument.

The job is still hard, though. Orchestras have music directors, whose style they get used to. Then they have guest conductors. (Imagine what it would be like if you had a different boss every few weeks!) Playing an instrument is both a physical and a mental task. You have to practice in order to keep your fingers, arms, and mouth in shape, and your technique at a high level. You need to deal with a wide range of repertoire. Most of all, you have to maintain your sense of yourself as a performing artist while you subordinate yourself to the group. A good conductor can make the players feel that their will and ideas are part of the performance —that they are not simply the tools of their egotistical leader.

My narrating career was going so well that I soon felt brave enough to resurrect my piano playing. Like the narrating, it had to be for some worthy cause, and eventually the right one came along. I was invited to perform with the famous Philadelphia Orchestra.

Normally, an amateur pianist wouldn't play with the Philadelphia Orchestra at the wonderful old Academy of Music, but this was a special occasion. It was the early 1970s, and the governor of Pennsylvania was running for reelection. He happened to be a pretty good amateur violinist, so he conceived a unique fundraiser. He hired not only the Academy of Music, but also about seventy members of the Philadelphia Orchestra, and also engaged the great Metropolitan Opera tenor Jan Peerce, whose singing I had so admired during my college opera forays. The house sold out at benefit prices: clearly, the idea was an improvement on the usual boring rubber chicken political dinner. Who wouldn't want to listen to music rather than speeches!

The governor played part of a concerto, and I played the slow movement of Mozart's Piano Concerto No. 21, that beautiful, lyrical piece that had been used as the theme of the movie *Elvira Madigan,* so everybody knew it. The reaction at that benefit was electric—a sigh of recognition went up from the audience. Even now, nearly twenty years after the movie came out, people still have a special response to that concerto, while Mozart, thanks in part to the movie *Amadeus* (which not only showed his raucous life but encouraged people to listen to his music and discover for themselves how stunning and varied it is), has become one of the most popular classical composers. Who would have thought that this child genius who played several instruments, toured Europe with his father and sister performing before royalty, told the archbishop of Salzburg what he could do with his job, wrote sublime music, and died in 1791 at the age of thirty-five would be the hit of the twentieth century?

Anyway, the *Elvira Madigan* concerto turned into something of a party piece for me. It was pretty, it was popular, and it was relatively easy to play, because it was slow and in the key of C, so I found myself invited to play it at benefits fairly regularly. Narrating was one thing. Playing the piano in public was a whole new ball game. I had done my little pieces while campaigning, but when I played a concerto, it was in a concert hall, with a full orchestra onstage behind me, and a house full of people out in front who were not talking and using me as background music but were there to listen.

Whenever I had to do one of these turns, I always found myself worrying about things that had nothing to do with the music. For example, I once bought a beautiful pair of shoes to go with a concert dress, and I only realized at the last moment that the heels were too high. Not only would I probably walk out onstage and turn an ankle, more importantly, I would probably have a hard time pedaling. And as anyone who plays the piano knows, when you panic, you put down the pedal because it creates a wash of sound that covers a multitude of sins. I ditched the shoes and got another pair that didn't match quite as well, and didn't feel right.

I don't know if it was the shoes that threw me off, but at that concert, a benefit at the Wang Center in Boston, I made my biggest performance flub. I still don't know how it happened. I'd played *Elvira Madigan* so many times that I could probably do it in my sleep, but in the middle of the piece, for some reason, I didn't see the conductor (Harry Ellis Dickson) cue me, and so I didn't come in. Two or three bars later, I realized that I'd blown it, and I had to make a split-second decision: do I try and figure out where we are and come in there, do I start my line from the beginning, or do I just stop and look helpless, so the whole thing gets started over? The last option is really bush league, and I didn't think I could manage the first, so I just started my entrance. I don't know how they did it, but Dickson and the musicians just jumped backward to where I was. (Musicians are incredible—opera orchestra musicians can follow singers no matter what they do.) Fortunately, on this occasion, the audience was a benefit crowd, people who were there to support Horizon House in Boston and probably to see Bob Hope, who was on in the second half, so they didn't notice. Only the *Boston Globe* reviewer, who is a good friend, mentioned (gently) in his review that there was a bit of a synchronization problem.

My piano playing wasn't limited to concerto appearances. While I was on the National Symphony board, I was asked to do another kind of benefit: a two-piano performance of the Darius Milhaud (1892–1974) *Scaramouche* with Antal Dorati, who was then the music director of the orchestra. The piece was Dorati's idea: it's very fast and lively, and he thought people would like it, so I said yes.

Fast and lively isn't really my strong suit. My repertoire is more in the slow and lyrical vein. What is more, *Scaramouche* is a fairly modern piece, and I'm more comfortable performing music from the eighteenth or early nineteenth century, such as Haydn, Mozart, or Chopin. *Scaramouche* has lots of chords, syncopated rhythms, and octaves, and I knew that it would require lots of finger dexterity and strong hands. What is more, there wouldn't be twenty violins coming in to cover me up: I'd have to pull my own weight and synchronize just right with my partner, who happened to be a famous conductor and the music director of Washington's orchestra. We were to be the entertainment for a dinner party for a thousand guests under a tent at a private house, and the guests were my peers on the board. No getting away with the unknowledgeable listener this time—these people were symphony subscribers, just like me.

But it was a challenge, and I like challenges. I was also flattered to be asked. I wasn't doing much playing at the time, just narrations, and I had no particular practice routine. Actually, I haven't had one since I was a child. Given my schedule, there was normally no point in setting aside a particular hour of the day to practice—I just did it when I could. If I didn't have to go out one afternoon, while the children were at school, I would get in a few hours. If a performance was coming up, other things simply had to go. This kind of flexibility has always worked best for me.

For *Scaramouche* I was up against it, so other things had to go. It took me a couple of months to get that piece down. As usual, I bought the record, put it on tape, and listened to it constantly. I started listening for my own part. It's one thing to practice your part over and over again, and I certainly did that, but you may have it down pat, get to the rehearsal (we had *one!*), and discover that the other person is in your way. So I played along with the record. Because I had the piece on tape, I was able to reverse and go over passages as often as I needed to.

I didn't disgrace myself, and everyone seemed pleased, including Dorati. Later I found out that he was even more frightened than I was. After all, here was a celebrated conductor who played the piano, but certainly not often or in public, performing for members of the board, who were technically his employers, and, even more frightening, before musicians from the orchestra over which he had to maintain authority and discipline. I was just an amateur with nothing to lose.

I did other kinds of piano performance. I once played a piano four-hands version of Dvořák's zippy, gypsy-inflected *Slavonic Dances* at the National Cathedral in Washington with the cathedral's organist. Piano four-hands is a lot easier than two-piano music, because both performers play the same piano. There's something very reassuring about being hip to hip with your collaborator (especially when he's doing the pedaling!) so he can nudge you if you're messing up.

But the most wonderful playing experience I had was before no audience at all. For several years on Sunday nights once a month, a small group of amateur players would get together to play chamber music at the home of David Lloyd Kreeger, who was chairman of the board of the National Symphony. David was a terrific violinist; Leonard Garment, the prominent lawyer, played clarinet, and Supreme Court Justice Abe Fortas also played the violin.

Chamber music is very special. It's probably one of the most rewarding things a player can do, because you have to play your own part but be exquisitely attuned to what two or three or four other players are doing at the same time. There is no conductor, and no one else is playing the same part you are. The lines weave together in a most wonderful, transparent way. String quartets can sound like one huge instrument with sixteen strings. When you add a piano, there's a new kind of bounce and buoyancy, and you have to be very careful not to drown out the strings. Put a clarinet, a violin, and a piano together, and you have three very different sonorities; each is heard on its own, but together they make something entirely new.

I wasn't nearly as good a pianist as my colleagues were at their instruments, so I usually practiced my part for a month before our meetings, while they could show up and sight-read and sound gorgeous. David and I would play sonatas by Handel, Vivaldi, and Mozart, and Leonard Garment would join us for trios.

David Kreeger was a collector, and his huge living room, hung with art, was acoustically wonderful. I had never really been aware of acoustics before, and how the size and shape of a room can make a difference in sound. We could hear each other beautifully in that room, and we were listening all the time, and watching for cues. Sometimes David, on first violin, had the lead; at other times, I did.

This was nothing like my narrations and piano solos. There was no getting dressed up, no extra rush from an audience, no huge waves of sound from an orchestra behind me. This was just a group of people getting together to play music because we loved it. Listening to music is wonderful, but nothing compares to making it yourself, and sharing that experience with other people.

The other side of my musical life in Washington was the creation of Joan Kennedy, classical music "groupie" extraordinaire. Great performers came to solo with the orchestra or play recitals, and I was there. I also found out that being a political wife is intimately bound up with entertaining. At parties and dinners—some of them scintillating, some of them otherwise—connections are made, and ideas set in motion. I used to say that one of the most important jobs of a senator's wife is to be able to converse with anybody for twenty minutes on a subject of burning importance to him or her, whether it is guerrillas in Central America,

World Bank loans to developing countries, or health care systems. I always knew who my dinner partners would be, or which party guests it was important for me to cultivate, and I did my homework.

But politicians get sick of just talking governmentese to each other, so the way to keep them happy is to invite glamorous or stimulating people from other professions to parties with them. Jackie Kennedy was brilliant at this, and her parties always "went," with their judicious mix of movie stars, playwrights, producers, and intellectuals to leaven the political lump. The government types were incredibly impressed by the stars, and vice versa. So I thought, why not put my love of music and musicians and my entertaining obligations together?

Since I was on the National Symphony board, it made perfect sense for me to give a reception for the orchestra's soloist after a concert. In 1966, Artur Rubinstein, the brilliant Polish-born pianist, was to give a solo recital in Washington. At the time, he was probably the best-known pianist in the world, known for his soulful interpretations of Chopin, who was always a favorite composer of mine. So I decided to give a party after the recital.

Ted wasn't as interested in classical music as I was, but he enjoyed my receptions. So after Rubinstein's Sunday afternoon recital, a select guest list—including the entire Senate Foreign Relations Committee, for whom we had gotten concert tickets—repaired to our townhouse in Georgetown for drinks and tea.

These were some of the top men in the Senate, most of them in their sixties: William Fulbright, John Stennis, and Claiborne Pell among them. Rubinstein arrived and was barely installed in a wing chair with his cup of tea when suddenly, all of these very important men had surrounded him and were hanging on his every word.

Spare and birdlike, with twinkling eyes, Rubinstein, who was nearly eighty at the time, was an unusually cultivated and intelligent man and an extraordinary raconteur. He took a lively interest in world affairs and was just back from Eastern Europe. With the Cold War at its height, and information hard to come by, the last person to visit was automatically the expert. Rubinstein was willing and well able to play the role. These senators, who thought they knew everything about foreign affairs, got what amounted to a briefing on the subject in the most entertaining and charming manner possible. Rubinstein never let them feel that he was one up on them, either.

People in Washington loved those parties. We'd have a buffet after the concert, starting at ten-thirty or eleven at night, and we'd always get forty or fifty guests—sometimes, I must admit, including people who hadn't made it to the concert but wanted to hang around with musicians. We had Rubinstein twice more, and the wonderful violinist Isaac Stern, who was also an articulate and amusing guest.

Many of my parties saluted young performers. There was Van Cliburn, of course, the tall, handsome Texan pianist who had won first prize at the Tchaikovsky competition in the Soviet Union in 1958. Cliburn, then twenty-three years old, was lionized by the Russians and, with the Cold War at its height, became an instant hero at home. Another favorite was the pianist André Watts, then in his twenties, and one of the few black artists to be on the superstar track. He had made a spectacular debut with Leonard Bernstein on a televised Young People's Concert when he was only sixteen, and then substituted for another pianist at the last minute on a regular Philharmonic subscription concert. Everyone wanted to meet these young celebrities.

I discovered I had a lot in common with all those politicians. I was totally star-struck, and I still am. I've met dozens

of great artists. Some of them, like Leonard Bernstein, Mstislav Rostropovich, and Yo-Yo Ma, became friends. Even if
they didn't, I still became a dedicated "groupie" in Washington, attending all their concerts (and rehearsals, sometimes),
going backstage afterward, having parties for them. I love
musicians, regardless of how famous they are. I always go
backstage at the Boston Symphony to talk to soloists,
whether I know them or not. I find that they're almost always pleased, especially the young ones who aren't famous
and don't have a huge entourage or a line of people waiting
to ask for their autographs. Soloists spend weeks and months
on the road, away from their families, and they are happy to
see people they know, or even friendly people they don't
know. Being a performer is lonely and difficult—imagine
having to psych yourself up to perform a challenging concerto or solo recital almost every night, far away from the
people who give you emotional support.

I love the whole notion of being behind the scenes in the
music world—in fact, I'd almost rather attend a rehearsal
than a concert. Everyone shows up in jeans and sneakers—
they're there to work things out. The conductor and the
soloist need to make sure that their ideas about tempi
(speeds) and dynamics (loudness and softness) mesh. They
may also have different interpretive ideas about a work. Try
singing a song or reading a passage from a book aloud. Then
ask someone else to do the same. You'll probably have two
entirely different interpretations of the same words or notes.
There are certain basic tenets for every work, or school, that
are established through research, but within those there are
all sorts of liberties.

Even the traditions change. In Victorian England, huge
choruses with hundreds of members used to perform Handel's oratorio *Messiah* with its famous "Hallelujah Chorus."
Today, scholars and performers look back to the way the

music was performed when Handel wrote it, and *Messiah* choruses may now have fewer than twenty singers. The "original instrument" movement has drastically changed interpretive attitudes about the music of Mozart and Haydn, for example. Players and conductors now often work with copies of seventeenth- and eighteenth-century instruments, like the ones that the composers used, and because the sounds they make are lighter and softer, the sound of the music is different—often faster, accented more like dance music. Imagine a violin soloist who plays with a big, Romantic sound working with a conductor who usually leads period instrument orchestras. They would have to work hard to come to a common ground.

That is a particularly drastic example, but in any case, a soloist may take liberties with the music on the page. An experienced conductor's skill is to follow the soloist, no matter what he or she does, and make the piece sound beautiful. I love watching an orchestra and soloist work through tricky passages in a movement, repeating them until they're right, skipping whole sections to get to the next problem spot, and then—the payoff—playing through the whole thing. Listening to the whole movement, I can pick out those former problem spots and see how they now fit seamlessly into the whole.

One of my favorite conductors was Leonard Bernstein. I met Lenny when Jack was President. They had been at Harvard together, and Jack and Jackie always used to ask him for musical advice. He was music director of the New York Philharmonic then, a brilliant man, magnetic and filled with energy. I loved to watch his rehearsals, because he didn't just correct, he instructed. He wouldn't just talk about dynamics, he'd talk about feelings, about what a particular phrase meant to him. Musicians don't always put up with that—they can get very focused on getting the job done without any extraneous emotion—but they didn't mind it from Lenny.

Lenny was a great talker, and someone with an amazingly wide range of interests, which came out in his music as well as his conversation. I love his music—not just the popular pieces, like *West Side Story* and *Candide,* but also works like the *Jeremiah* Symphony and the beautiful *Chichester Psalms.* I went to see his *Mass* four times. *Mass* was written for the opening of the Kennedy Center in Washington in 1971. It was a real effort to fuse the popular culture and upheavals of the 1960s with the traditional Latin mass, and it has everything in it but the kitchen sink—ancient church music, symphonic tone poem, modern rock and roll, and a pure, heartfelt ballad, "A Simple Song." I think Bernstein understood more about the Catholic Church than most Catholics do. Some of the piece came off, some of it didn't, but Bernstein certainly wore his heart on his sleeve, and he shared it with everyone.

I saw Lenny nearly every summer at Tanglewood, the Boston Symphony's summer home in western Massachusetts, where he went to teach and conduct. A few years ago, they threw a big seventieth birthday bash for him—it went on for days—and after his big concert of the weekend, there was a party up at Saranac, the house that belonged to Serge Koussevitzky, the conductor who founded Tanglewood and championed Bernstein as a conductor and a composer fifty years ago. The supper started at eleven, and Lenny decided he wanted to see the sun come up, so the party never ended. He entertained us all night with stories about music, travel, politics, and people. He died unexpectedly in 1990, and it's still hard to believe that he's gone.

A high public profile has its uses. Feting musicians, narrating with orchestras, and playing charity concerts were fun for me, but as Ted Kennedy's wife I also had the chance to do a good turn for someone in the music world who needed it badly.

In April 1974, Ted, Teddy Jr., Kara, and I were slated to travel to the Soviet Union. As the family culture vulture, I was naturally planning to seek out prominent Soviet artists and visit cultural institutions. Suggestions abounded. There was, of course, the Bolshoi Ballet and Opera. Among the people who might be visited were the violinist David Oistrakh, the composer Sergei Prokofiev's widow, and the pianist Emil Gilels, who in 1955 had been the first Soviet artist to play in America under the Cold War exchanges. Then I got a message from Leonard Bernstein about Slava Rostropovich.

Mstislav Rostropovich, the world-renowned Russian cellist and conductor, was at the time living a nightmare in his own country. In 1969, Rostropovich invited the writer Aleksandr Solzhenitsyn, who was in disfavor with the government and living in poverty, to live in his dacha, or country house, outside Moscow. Government officials told him to evict Solzhenitsyn, and they made life difficult for him when he refused. In 1970 Rostropovich, determined to make his position clear, wrote a letter supporting Solzhenitsyn—who had been awarded the Nobel Prize and was being attacked in the press—to the Soviet newspapers. It was at once published abroad, and the repercussions were swift. Slava's tours abroad and at home were cancelled. His wife, the celebrated soprano Galina Vishnevskaya, also suffered, losing her leading roles and recording assignments. Friends, fearing to associate with the couple, shunned them. Solzhenitsyn was exiled after several years, but Rostropovich and Vishnevskaya remained, frightened and humiliated. Their careers and lives in a shambles, the pair finally applied for visas to emigrate in March 1974.

Word had begun to filter out to the West about what was happening to Rostropovich. The official story, which no one believed, was that his tours and concerts were being cancelled because he was ill. Lenny and Felicia Bernstein, who knew him, were worried, and they saw our trip as an opportunity to see him, find out what was going on, and at least boost his morale.

With the help of Harry Kraut, who worked with Lenny, a "Slava plan" evolved. The first idea was for me to send Slava a letter in Russian from Kiev, where we were supposed to stop first, asking him to contact me in Moscow. This little subterfuge, using internal mail to avoid government interception and suspicion, was foiled when our plans changed and we went directly to Moscow.

So I had to try something else. The Soviet Union under Brezhnev was very cloak-and-dagger: if Ted and I had something to talk about that we didn't want the KGB to know, we went into the bathroom of our government residence and talked with the water running. But I thought that maybe the direct approach might be just what was needed—there's value in publicity, after all. So I went to the Moscow Conservatory, where Rostropovich was supposed to be teaching, and asked for him. I asked *everyone* about him. I was told he was ill, but I just kept asking, assuming that word would get around. Of course it did: to Madame Yekaterina Furtseva, the powerful minister of culture, and from her to the top, Brezhnev himself.

The following day, Ted had his private visit with Brezhnev. The statesman's wife always goes along for the introductions and a little preliminary socializing, but just as it is in good old American campaign politics, I was supposed to look nice, be friendly, and not say anything untoward—not say anything at all, really.

Brezhnev knew the script too. He asked me politely if I

was enjoying Moscow, and if there was anything that he could do to make it better. I hadn't thought this out in advance, but it came to me that it was now or never. I took a deep breath and, feeling like the humble subject begging a favor of a king who might order me hauled off to execution, said that I wanted to meet Slava Rostropovich and invite him personally to come and conduct the National Symphony, of which I was on the board of directors. Of course (I piled it on), this would be at the Kennedy Center, which had recently been opened and dedicated to my late brother-in-law.

Ted looked at me as though I had suddenly gone completely mad. Brezhnev looked surprised too, though probably more at the breach of protocol than the request, for which he must have been prepared, but he smoothly replied that he had heard of my inquiries at the conservatory and would consider my request. Brezhnev probably took this public incident as a useful opportunity to resolve the Rostropovich situation, which was becoming embarrassing for his government. Rostropovich and his wife got their exit visas two days later. He left the country in May; she followed in July with their daughters.

Slava did come to conduct the National Symphony—he became its music director in 1977, and he still is. He and Galina were stripped of their Soviet citizenship and the titles ("People's Artist of the USSR" and the like) which count for so much there, and he became something of a symbol of artistic freedom here. It was only in 1990 that things had changed enough in the Soviet Union for the government to restore Slava's citizenship, and for him to go back, with the National Symphony, for a visit.

I never actually saw Slava on that trip, but I certainly saw a great deal of him later. Recently, I caught up with him in New York, where he was rehearsing a new concerto by Alfred Schnittke, a famous contemporary Soviet composer, with the Boston Symphony. The orchestra was in sweatshirts and jeans; Slava—always formal and correct, in a business suit with a pale blue shirt that matched his eyes—played through this mournful and very challenging work (for players and audience alike) with absolute concentration and panache. Backstage in his dressing room, he introduced me to the tiny, yippy dog that he takes everywhere with him (it has its own little zipped carrier that Slava slings over his shoulder), and he told me what his situation was like that April.

"After we made our request for exit visas, Galina and I went to a meeting with the deputy minister of culture, who asked why I wanted to leave. I told him, 'You know better than I what the reason is. You cancel my concerts, take me out of the Bolshoi. Cancel everything, and I have no life.' He laughed and smiled and said, 'You know, you want to play with the orchestra, but maybe the orchestra doesn't want to play with you.' Galina said, 'That's exactly why we want to leave, because we know that in New York, Philadelphia, and Boston, the orchestras will want to play with him.' Then I had a rehearsal with the Operetta Theater. Afterwards, the director told me to come to his office, and told me that the premiere was to be cancelled. I asked him why. He said, 'Honestly, because you are not so great a musician as you once were.'

"I didn't say a word. I left his office and had hysterics. I cried like a child. April was the most terrible month. On the one hand, people were telling us that the government was going to let us leave. On the other, we didn't know what would happen. Maybe they would put us in prison, maybe kill us. When I went into the conservatory, professors would stare at the wall, just so they wouldn't have to greet me. That was what the atmosphere was like when suddenly, there was a telephone call, and a voice, with a strong accent and not very good Russian, said, 'Maestro Rostropovich? I am here with Senator Kennedy. And I want you to know that today Senator Kennedy and the General Secretary had three hours of conversation, and one of the matters they spoke about was you.' "

After Slava and I talked, he packed the little dog into the purse and closed up his cello case, and we walked out the back door of Carnegie Hall. We said our goodbyes—very Russian, lots of hugs and kisses—and he turned left, toward the Parker Meridien Hotel down the block. I turned right, but I stopped and looked back. It was lunch hour, and crowds of people were pouring down 56th Street. Nobody recognized him; nobody made way for him as he made his way down the street, pushing that huge cello case on its wheels. He had some trouble getting the wheels over the bumps in the pavement, so he seemed to weave along, almost swimming upstream, looking rather frail, and a good ten years older than he is. It seemed so ironic. He's a famous artist; people come to his concerts, buy his records, crowd him backstage, demand his autograph, give him standing ovations. But at the end of the performance, after the crowds go home, there's always that loneliness, no matter who you are.

The wonderful thing about all these friendships is that they survived the end of my life as a political wife. Indeed, my immersion in music as a performer, a fan, and a friend is one of the things that gave me strength. When Ted and I divorced in 1984, I was narrating regularly and enjoying it a lot. Being a politician's wife involves a lot of reflected glory, and sometimes I wondered if people had any idea that I had any personality of my own, apart from being Ted's wife. Of course, I *started* narrating because I was a senator's wife, but orchestras asked me back because I did a good job. I was professional and the conductor didn't have to worry that I would miss cues. This was my own province, and I was proud of it.

But when I ceased to be a senator's wife, I assumed that my career was over. Although I had moved to Boston in 1981 when Ted and I separated, and I was starting to feel as though it was my home town too, Boston was still the Kennedy stronghold city, and I was sure that the Boston Symphony wouldn't want me to narrate anymore now that we were divorced. So I was touched when John Williams, who became the Pops conductor after Arthur Fiedler died, invited me to narrate. Not only did he ask me, he agreed to do Britten's *Young Person's Guide* instead of *Peter and the Wolf* (which I was heartily sick of by that point), even though he had never conducted it before. He made me feel like a pro, trusting me to get through the piece without needing much help from him.

John Williams is a modest man with immense talent and a great sweetness about him. He doesn't take himself too seriously, and he's a wonderful entertainer—I once watched him during the filming of a Pops concert for television, and he ad-libbed jokes and stories for the audience to keep everyone amused between shots. He endeared himself to me right away. Just a few weeks after that performance of the Britten, which went very well, I was down at Hyannis Port on Cape Cod for the Fourth of July weekend when John called me. A soloist had cancelled—could I come up to Boston and narrate for the big open-air concert on the Esplanade? He was most concerned about inconveniencing me, but I couldn't believe my luck. He didn't have to ask twice. I was in the car and in Boston within hours, and in the Esplanade band shell, feeling the warm breezes off the Charles River, with thousands of people lying on blankets on the grass and listening to us perform, I had one of the happiest evenings of my life.

FIVE

A Short History
of Classical Music

MUSIC HAS BEEN A PART of human expression
from earliest recorded history. Egyptian tomb
paintings and Greek urns show people playing
flutes, drums, and lyres. Pick any civilization on the planet
today, and you'll find indigenous music and instruments: the
thumb pianos and talking drums of Central Africa, the panpipes of the Andes, Indonesian gamelans, Indian ragas, and
more recent, hybrid strains, such as American jazz.

In this book, I am dealing specifically with one stream of
music, which for want of a better term is usually called
Western classical or concert music. Born as folk and church
music in Europe, changed and developed over nine centuries
or so by countless composers, some famous, some anony-
mous, it has become an internationally known and practiced
language. The story of this music is rich and complex. Every
country had its own composers, styles, and specialties. Some

composers flowered in isolation, others influenced and were influenced by the music of foreigners. The full history of Western music requires books of its own; my aim here is to give a taste of the story—its flavor and sequence—and some of my favorite pieces within it. I certainly can't mention everyone—I can't even include everyone important—but here's a start.

Since I'm talking favorites, I need to begin closer to the end than to the beginning of the history. The music I love the best was written late in the nineteenth century, a time when the symphony orchestra, one of the principal media of this music, had been developed to the enormous size and complexity we know today. There's something so amazing to me about seeing more than a hundred musicians sitting onstage, perfectly coordinated, displaying an extraordinary variety of sound. When a soloist joins them, there is the added excitement of contrast and competition between the one and the many. The Romantic period of the nineteenth century, which gave birth to poets like Lord Byron, Percy Bysshe Shelley, and William Wordsworth, also fostered a musical outpouring of feeling, and the orchestra, with its splendid palette, was the perfect vehicle for the composers of that time. I'm a pushover for the Romantic concertos and symphonies.

To give you an idea of what Romantic expression was all about, consider the Russian composer Piotr Ilyich Tchaikovsky (1840–93). Moody, emotional, tormented by the homosexuality that he dared not acknowledge, Tchaikovsky wrote monumental symphonies and concertos and fairy-tale ballets. His Piano Concerto No. 1 (1875) is a favorite of mine, and also of pianists who revel in big statements. If you've ever heard the song "Tonight We Love," you know the first movement's big theme. It's a huge, sweeping tune, and as the orchestra plays it, the pianist crashes out chords that turn the heaviest beats into a thunder of sound.

Everything is big about this concerto. Its first movement is nearly twenty minutes long, its orchestral accompaniment stresses mass and power rather than any individual orchestral section or instrument, and the pianist's alternately heroic and hysterical struggle up the scale creates an almost unbearable tension. Yet there is playfulness in the concerto too—there are rippling piano figures and a gentle three-minute cadenza (in which the pianist plays alone). Indeed, that big first theme never comes back in the concerto's entire thirty-five minutes: Tchaikovsky had plenty of other ideas, and he spun them out, weaving them loosely into the concerto's fabric. It certainly confused musicians when it was written: when Tchaikovsky took the piece to his friend and mentor, the conductor Nicolai Rubinstein, Rubinstein declared it unplayable, clumsily written, and trivial. He has, of course, since been proved wrong.

The Romantic concerto—and the big orchestra that plays it, now the centerpiece of international concert life—is only one step along the continuum that started with flutes, lyres, and singing and today includes electronics and sound combinations that Tchaikovsky probably never imagined in his wildest dreams. But when you compare nineteenth-century symphonies to the music of the Middle Ages and the Renaissance, they seem to be from different planets. Much early music is vocal. It has its own textures and dynamics, and it is played on instruments that bear only a passing resemblance to their modern counterparts. It was written for use in churches, celebrations, and entertainments, and it was not necessarily intended to be passed down to succeeding generations. Unlike the symphonies and quartets of the eighteenth, nineteenth, and twentieth centuries, it is very loosely notated.

An orchestra playing Tchaikovsky's piano concerto has a detailed score and therefore knows exactly how many instruments are required, and what notes, in what rhythm, and at what basic speed each one will play. In much earlier music, many of these elements are left to the players' discretion—the exact instrumental complement is often unspecified, for example. Musicians who specialize in such music today have to be researchers as well as performers. They examine the ancient documents and treatises explaining what the musical style was, and what the music sounded like, and then they reconstruct it by following those clues. Performing on replicas of instruments copied from books and paintings, they recreate a vanished world.

The voice is the most natural instrument that exists, and vocal music is how music history began. In the Middle Ages, clerics sang unaccompanied Gregorian chant as part of the Christian mass, and minstrels wandered the countryside entertaining the nobility and the peasants alike with heroic epics, dramatic ballads, and love songs. Songs and dances were accompanied by harps, bowed instruments called vielles (predecessors of the modern violin), zithers, lutes, wooden flutes, trumpets, and drums. Melodies were at first improvised and passed on by demonstration, but by the eleventh century, composed tunes were notated, and so they could be communicated more accurately from composer to player. At the same time, composers began to combine melodies so that two or more independent voices could sound simultaneously, a technique called polyphony. Composers, like the people who built the cathedrals of the Middle Ages, were considered craftsmen doing their jobs, rather than artists creating works for the ages, and few of their names have come down to us.

Like the other arts, music flourished in the Renaissance (roughly 1450–1600). Composers broadened their scope, and printing enabled many more people to participate in musical performance. Vocal music, created for the church by composers like the Flemish Johannes Ockeghem (c. 1410–97), the Flemish Josquin Des Prez (c. 1440–1521), the Italian Giovanni Palestrina (c. 1525–94), and the English William Byrd (1543–1623), became increasingly complex and virtuosic. In the secular realm, composers like the Italian Claudio Monteverdi (1567–1643) and the Englishman John Dowland (1562–1626) brought the madrigal, a polyphonic vocal form, to great heights. Instrumental sophistication increased as well. Instruments were built in families which enabled a single timbre (that of the recorder or viol, for instance) to be sounded from the very highest soprano to the lowest bass note. The consort of viols—fretted, six-stringed instruments played upright—would be played on their own, a philosophy closer to the modern string quartet than to the modern orchestra, which has the full range of stringed instruments but specializes in combining and contrasting that string sound with other timbres. Solo instruments, like the harpsichord (predecessor of the piano), organ, and lute (ancestor of the guitar), gained prominence.

The earliest era with which most modern musicians and audiences are very familiar is the Baroque (1600–1750). The forms—opera, concerto, symphony, sonata—that were to dominate the ensuing centuries were codified then. Instruments, too, began to approach the forms that they now have, as the soft-voiced viol family gave way to the more piercing, four-string violin family, for example. Composers began to write for specific instruments and voices.

Italy was a major center of musical development during the Baroque period. In Florence, for example, opera as we know it today was born when a small group of musical aesthetes, the Florentine Camerata, decided to re-create the ancient Greek combination of music and drama. One stunning result was the operas of Claudio Monteverdi. His *Orfeo,* first performed in 1607 and based on the Orpheus and Eurydice story, featured solo airs, ensembles, a poignant chorus, and a huge (for the time), expressive orchestra of forty instruments. Opera became extremely popular in Italy, and later in England and in France, where Jean-Baptiste Lully and Jean-Philippe Rameau wrote elaborate opera-ballets for the court of Louis XIV. Italy also gave its language to music, as France did to ballet: *piano* (meaning "soft"), *allegro* (meaning "fast"), and the like are the international speech of composers, conductors, and musicians.

One of the greatest composers of opera in the Italian style in the eighteenth century was, curiously enough, a German, George Frideric Handel (1685–1759), who wrote many of his greatest works for London—a prime example of international cross-fertilization. In Handel's day, highly trained, virtuosic singers, adored by the public in the way that rock and pop stars are today, performed his operas. Each solo song (aria) was an opportunity to communicate a particular emotion. Baroque composers developed the da capo ("from the top") aria, which consisted of an opening section, a middle section that set a contrasting mood, and finally a repeat of the opening section, which would be sung with different emphasis, and with vocal frills and ornaments that would stun the listeners. Many such arias would be stitched together with information that advanced the plot, sung over a simple accompaniment (recitative). Giving every character in the opera the opportunity to advance his or her point of view in da capo form made for a long evening. But Handel's operas, once considered hopelessly long and static when compared to those that followed them, are enjoying a revival today as singers discover the excitement of the vocal challenges that so thrilled eighteenth-century audiences.

When the vogue for Italian opera died in London, Handel, who had a living to make, turned to the creation of oratorios—large works for orchestra, chorus, and soloists on Biblical subjects—such as the ever popular *Messiah*. Handel was also kept busy creating music for special events, such as court outings on the Thames River. In such an event, the royal barge would be surrounded by scores of boats, including one containing musicians who performed Handel's specially composed suites entitled *Water Music*.

The Baroque period was also the cauldron that saw the birth of orchestral forms as we know them today. The instrumental sinfonia of the opera would eventually give birth to the symphony; composers were beginning to work with forms in which solo instruments or groups of solo instruments alternated with an ensemble—the concerto. The king of the Baroque concerto was Antonio Vivaldi (1678–1741) of Venice. Vivaldi, who once bragged that he could compose a complete concerto in less time than would be required to copy it, wrote about 500 concertos, more than 230 of them for violin. These include one of my favorite Baroque pieces: *The Four Seasons* (1725), a collection of four concertos.

Trained as both a violinist and a priest, Vivaldi spent nearly his entire working life directing musical activities at the Conservatory of the Pietà in Venice, a religious institution for orphan girls. Venice was an extremely musical city, and Vivaldi's girls, trained to be an accomplished orchestra, chorus, and soloists, as well as the music he constantly wrote for them, made their church services in Venice into a popular destination for Venetians and foreigners alike. Visitors carried news of Vivaldi's achievements abroad, and his own fairly constant travels made him a powerful influence on his contemporaries and those who followed him.

The concertos of *The Four Seasons* barely need the little sonnets that were published with them to establish what they are about. The joyful, quicksilver opening of *Spring,* with its ominous rumblings of a distant thunderstorm, sets the scene quite clearly, as does the languid *Summer,* the revelries of *Autumn,* and the icy nullity of *Winter.* You can't get much further in character from Tchaikovsky's concerto of 150 years later. The movements are short, mostly around three minutes (you'll recall that the first movement of Tchaikovsky's First Piano Concerto runs twenty minutes), and the textures are thin and clear. The forms, too, are clear, giving the soloist a solid framework in which to go crazy. Each concerto has three movements with contrasting moods and speeds (fast-slow-fast), and the soloist alternates with the orchestra, which is small and made up entirely of strings. The soloist engages in wilder and wilder flights of musical fancy, but no matter how far afield he or she goes, the theme always returns (this is called "ritornello" or rondo form).

Meanwhile, Johann Sebastian Bach (1685–1750) was a musician for hire, first in various German courts, and for his last 27 years as director of music for the Lutheran St. Thomas's church school in Leipzig. St. Thomas's fifty-five boys sang and played for four churches in the city of Leipzig, and Bach wrote the music they performed. Like Vivaldi, he wrote music for use—works for organ, harpsichord, and instrumental ensembles for his aristocrats. In Leipzig, he wrote hundreds of cantatas (works for chorus, soloists, and small instrumental ensemble based on Biblical texts), as the churches required fifty-eight of them a year, plus Passions for Easter week. Bach was the master of polyphony and complexity, combining multiple musical lines into great fugues, yet speaking directly to God with the mighty chorales of his Passions.

In the late eighteenth century, music moved further out of the churches and into public concert halls and the drawing rooms of the middle class. The Enlightenment touched the composers of the Classical period (1750–1800) as well as its writers. The extravagant, virtuosic effects of the Baroque period were to be abandoned in favor of simplicity and humanism. Classicists wished to return to what they saw as the purity and wisdom of ancient civilizations—balance and serenity were the ideals.

Orchestras grew up in European—especially Austrian and German—cities. They were not the dozen or so stringed instruments that Vivaldi worked with, but a string complement balanced by two each of oboes, flutes, clarinets, bassoons, trumpets, horns, and timpani, and sometimes a harpsichord. Soon the harpsichord disappeared from the orchestra, and its player, who formerly led the musicians, was replaced in his leadership function by the head of the first violins—and later by a conductor. By the end of the century, orchestras might have as many as thirty-five players; some orchestras, depending on local resources, might have even more. At the same time, the harpsichord was falling out of fashion altogether, replaced by the new "fortepiano" (literally "loud-soft"), in which the instrument's strings were struck by hammers rather than plucked by quills, providing it with dynamic range impossible on the harpsichord.

The old opera "sinfonia"—a short instrumental preface or interlude that offered a rest from the serious business of opera, namely singing—developed into something quite new: the symphony. It became popular too—a catalogue of symphonies written between 1720 and 1810 lists 12,350, but the center of symphonic composition was Vienna, where Haydn, Mozart, and then Beethoven became the titans of Classical composition.

Franz Joseph Haydn (1732–1809), father of the modern symphony, was the last major composer to depend on patronage. In 1761, he entered into thirty years of service to the aristocratic Esterházy family, much of the time spent at their country estate in what is now Hungary. At Esterháza, with its two theaters and two music rooms, its orchestra of twenty-five players (built up by Haydn) and complement of singers, Haydn had his work cut out for him. He had to write a lot—two operas and two long concerts were presented each week, and new music was expected for all of them. Cut off from the world, he said, "There was no one around to mislead and harass me, and so I was forced to become original." Like Vivaldi's, however, his works spread abroad, gathering fame and establishing a profound influence on the musical world from which he had been shut away. When Haydn was sixty, the new Esterházy ruler lost interest in music, so Haydn, backed by an impresario, traveled to London, where he wrote the most influential of his 104 symphonies. (The string quartet also owes a profound debt to Haydn—he wrote 68 of them).

In Haydn's hands, the symphony developed from a form that was considered fairly light music, not as significant as concertos or operas, into a freestanding, serious work. Its four-movement form provided a particular structure. First movements were relatively fast-paced, with the meat of the thematic material; second movements were slow arias, melodic and contrasting. The third movements, minuets, were explicitly based on the dance form, and they were succeeded by exciting finales that balanced the importance of the first movement.

The basic first-movement form, called sonata form, is one of the hallmarks of the Classical style, but imaginative composers took liberties with it. In sonata form, the movement begins with a theme, which is repeated. It is then developed —the composer plays around with the theme—and finally repeated at the end, often with a little tag called a "coda." Sonata form is indigenous to sonatas (solo instrumental works), quartets, trios, and other chamber music, as well as symphonies.

By the time Haydn was writing his London symphonies, Mozart was already dead, having left an indelible mark on the history of music. In 1785, Haydn told Leopold Mozart, "I must tell you before God and as an honest man that your son is the greatest composer I ever heard of." Born in Salzburg, Austria, Wolfgang Amadeus Mozart (1756–91) was a prodigy. Trained by Leopold, Wolfgang wrote his first minuets when he was six and his first opera when he was twelve, and he spent a good part of his childhood performing all over Europe. These performances were not concerts as we know them today: young Wolfgang would sit at the keyboard sight-reading whatever music was put in front of him, or asking for a tune and then improvising around it, as well as playing his own compositions. These travels exposed him to the musical styles of all of Europe: he took what he wanted and made it his own. Mozart's father sought a court post for him, but Mozart was not suited to the courtier's life, and he spent his last ten years as a freelance composer in Vienna, sometimes short of cash but always a source of awe to his contemporaries. When he died, one of them said of him, "It is a pity to lose so great a genius, but a good thing for us that he is dead. For if he had lived much longer, we should not have earned a crust of bread by our compositions."

The movie *Amadeus* brought Mozart's tempestuous life and early death to modern audiences. Like thousands of other Americans, I ran out and bought recordings of his music after seeing the movie, and I developed a greater appreciation of his genius than I had ever had before. His legacy—835 works, including 41 symphonies, 54 solo concertos, 21 operas, and 98 chamber music works—is doubly astonishing when you consider that he was only thirty-five when he died. In that brief span, he composed in every medium, raising the piano concerto—one of the most serious media of the day—to new and eloquent heights, while at the same time creating stylish and beautiful serenades and divertimenti, like *Eine kleine Nachtmusik*. He took the old Italian opera form and infused it with a new sense of character, emotion, and plot in operas like *The Marriage of Figaro, Don Giovanni,* and *The Magic Flute*. Composing was not a struggle for Mozart: his mind and ears were full of ideas. Humor and sorrow, darkness and light—they exist side by side in Mozart's music, all spelled out with the most exquisite clarity, and with a genius for melody.

Mozart's symphonies are like his operas—full of emotion, both joy and suffering. His Symphony No. 41 (*Jupiter*), written in 1788, is a case in point. The first movement seems to grab you by the collar and demand your attention; the second, a mournful melody, is interrupted by an anguished cry that never seems to be answered. It keeps breaking into the melody, but the ending of the movement is quiet, with a calm resignation. Musically, matters may be resolved; emotionally they are not. Not all Mozart's contemporaries were as admiring as Haydn: many considered his music "too highly spiced" and revolutionary. Later generations prettified Mozart into a salon composer of tinkling melodies; more recent wisdom has restored him to his full complexity.

Modern audiences seem to have domesticated Ludwig van Beethoven (1770–1827), who was a bona fide revolutionary in his day. His nine symphonies are one of the cornerstones of the standard repertoire. The Ninth Symphony—with its finale based on Friedrich von Schiller's "Ode to Joy," using chorus and soloists—was a radical departure from established symphonic form; today it is one of the world's most popular works, especially in Japan, where it receives thousands of reverent performances each year. His late string quartets are challenging even to modern audiences.

Beethoven's life and struggles are the stuff of legend. Too stubborn to put up with any patron, he put on his own concerts and wrote for himself and for posterity. He said, "It is well to mingle with aristocrats, but one must know how to impress them." Beethoven wrote with difficulty (consider his nine symphonies, as opposed to Mozart's forty-one, or his five piano concertos—Mozart wrote twenty-seven). He first noticed signs of impending deafness in 1798; by 1820, his hearing loss was total, yet he continued to compose.

Beethoven's scores, with their volcanic energy, mirror his personal struggles and his striving to stretch the confines of the Classical style to the breaking point. He expanded sonata form to unheard-of proportions. When the quartet charged with performing his first Op. 59 (*Rasumovsky*) quartet got the score, they thought it was a joke. His thirty-two piano sonatas trace his development: it is easy to follow sonata form in the first movement of No. 8, the *Pathétique;* later sonatas are huge compendia of material. The last movement of the famous Symphony No. 9 runs an incredible twenty-five minutes and has nine different sections, ranging from a tub-thumping, comic town band to the huge choral outburst of Schiller's poem—which, written in a revolutionary age, is as much about freedom (*Freiheit*) as it is about joy (*Freude*), the word used in the text.

With his mighty struggles, Beethoven was a hero to the Romantics. For the worm had turned once again. Instead of balance, clarity, and formal perfection, extravagance and the yearning of the individual were back in vogue. Some composers clung to the forms of the past as they expanded their emotional output; others altered them beyond recognition.

Franz Schubert (1797–1828) was no thunderer, nor did he have Beethoven's attention-getting gifts. Schubert wrote nine symphonies, which had little recognition in his lifetime. His most appreciative audience was a circle of friends—writers, artists, musicians, bourgeois—who loved him and organized evenings devoted to his music that became known as "Schubertiades." Not surprisingly, he produced quantities of chamber music, dances, and songs (*Lieder* in German); in 1815 alone, Schubert wrote 144 songs.

Schubert's exquisite *Trout* Quintet (1819), for piano, violin, viola, cello, and double bass, displays Schubert's gift for melody and intimacy. Its fourth movement is based on one of his songs, "Die Forelle" (The Trout), and is a series of variations on that lovely melody, which, with its rippling figures, seems to picture a fish darting in a stream.

Two very different composers, Chopin and Liszt, revolutionized piano composition in the Romantic era. Their piano, a more technically advanced instrument than Mozart's, had more volume, dynamic range, and control, and they looked to the piano to express ideas for which other composers required the resources of the full orchestra.

Frédéric Chopin (1810–49), born in Poland, arrived in Paris in 1831 at the height of the Romantic movement. Young, graceful, with perfect manners, and fragile due to the tuberculosis that would finally kill him, Chopin became the toast of the town: he was called "a species of musical Wordsworth." He hated performing and soon stopped playing in public entirely, making his living teaching piano to aristocratic, if not always gifted, ladies for extremely high fees. A member of the lively artists' circle of the period, in 1838 he began a liaison with the female writer George Sand, which is detailed in her novels.

Chopin wrote almost exclusively for piano, expanding its sonorities and opening up the old forms into extended fantasias and diabolical scherzos. He wrote dozens of short pieces —nocturnes, preludes, mazurkas, waltzes, impromptus— that were easy enough for his students to play, yet inventive enough to display his own gifts. I find these little jewels to be the essence of Chopin—intimate and gentle, with singing melodies, tempos, and rhythms discreetly stretched, the sustaining pedal applied for a wash of sound. I especially love the two waltzes—Op. 64, Nos. 2 and 3—which are brief but create their own little sound worlds. The first, a famous one, makes me want to dance; the second, more rhythmically varied, would confound any dancer who tried. Then there are the nocturnes—slow, still, and hypnotic.

Franz Liszt (1811–86), on the contrary, was nothing if not a showman—a glamorous virtuoso, adored and worshipped like those eighteenth-century singers. Born in Hungary, he was a traveling piano virtuoso from the age of eleven. In contrast to Chopin—who, according to a contemporary observer, "carried you into a dreamworld" with his playing—Liszt was "all sunshine and dazzling splendor" with something diabolical about him as well. Two aristocratic women left their husbands to live with him; the first had three out-of-wedlock children with Liszt. Yet for all his flamboyance, Liszt was generous to other composers: as the music director at the Weimar court in Germany from 1848 until 1861, he championed the music of Richard Wagner and others.

Like Chopin, Liszt was based in Paris, where he heard the Italian violinist Niccolò Paganini perform astonishing pyrotechnics, and he resolved that he would do the same for the piano. Liszt wrote music for himself to play, and his long fingers could stretch to encompass tenths on the piano (ten white keys, about nine inches apart on a modern piano) as easily as others could play octaves (eight keys, about seven inches), making his music a formidable challenge for pianists. His B-minor Sonata has nothing to do with sonata form at all. It is a wide-ranging fantasy. Themes are introduced, changed, suppressed. The piano is an orchestra. There are huge contrasts—the left hand pounds out rhythms at the bottom of the keyboard, while the right hand trills delicately at the top. In his music, Liszt seems to be leading the listener through a tangled jungle, and only he knows the path.

The symphonists had a field day with Romanticism too. The symphonies and overtures of Felix Mendelssohn (1809–47) look back to Classical models yet evoke Romantic landscapes—consider his overture to *A Midsummer Night's Dream,* written when he was only seventeen. Mendelssohn, like many of his contemporaries, went to older models in search of inspiration: his performance of Bach's *St. Matthew Passion* in Berlin in 1829 reawakened interest in the composer, who had been forgotten for a century.

Robert Schumann (1810–56), who was also a pianist and married to another distinguished pianist, Clara Wieck, had something of a romantic career himself: he went mad and died in an asylum. I'm especially partial to his piano music, and to his Cello Concerto, which my friend Yo-Yo Ma introduced me to. Johannes Brahms (1833–97) who was also a pianist and was in love with Clara, wrote lush chamber music, including three beautiful piano quartets, four great symphonies, and four concertos—two for piano, one for violin (1878), and one for violin and cello (1887)—that are some of my favorites in the repertoire. Brahms had no fear of the big orchestra—its glowing colors reached new heights in his hands.

In France, Hector Berlioz (1803–69), transformed the symphony as Liszt had the sonata. (Liszt made some of his own transformations in the symphonic genre too.) His *Symphonie fantastique,* written in 1830, has five movements instead of the usual four and was published with a detailed description of the events each movement was depicting. The piece is a feverish imagining of an artist in the throes of unrequited love: in the whirl of *A Ball* (the second movement), he is obsessed with the woman he loves; in *March to*

I have chosen these photos from my personal collection to highlight my lifelong love of singing, dancing, and performing.

My parents nurtured my love of classical music; it was always playing on their radio at home, and they encouraged my piano playing and other musical activities. Here we sit before our Christmas tree at our home in Bronxville, when I was nine years old. From left, my father, Harry Wiggin Bennett; me; my sister, Candy; and my mother, Virginia Stead Bennett. (Author's collection)

In my Girl Scout uniform, age twelve, the year I started playing the violin in the high school orchestra. (Author's collection)

At my wedding to Ted Kennedy in 1958: my father is between my sister Candy and me; my mother is at right. (Author's collection)

I've always loved dance, in all its forms. Here I am dancing at my wedding with the best man, Jack Kennedy, as his brother Bobby Kennedy asks Jack if he can cut in. (Author's collection)

Music was also a big part of the Kennedy family's life. For Joseph Kennedy's birthdays we would serenade him with songs of our own devising. Here we are in Hyannis Port, summer 1962: from left: me; Eunice Shriver; Jackie Kennedy; Ethel Kennedy; Jean Smith; Ted Kennedy; Bobby Kennedy; President Kennedy; and Steve Smith. (Author's collection)

In December 1967, I appeared with Arthur Fiedler and the National Symphony in Washington to narrate Prokofiev's *Peter and the Wolf*. Here I wait for Maestro Fiedler to give me my cue. (Author's collection)

After I had performed, I joined my sister Candy and my children, Teddy Jr. and Kara, to sing Christmas carols with the orchestra. (Author's collection)

CONCERT

The Arts Committee for SHAPP/KLINE presents:

MRS. EDWARD (JOAN)
KENNEDY
WORLD PIANO DEBUT

JAN
PEERCE
METROPOLITAN OPERATIC TENOR

MEMBERS OF THE
PHILADELPHIA ORCHESTRA
SIXTEEN CONCERTO SOLOISTS
CONDUCTED BY **WILLIAM SMITH** ASSISTANT CONDUCTOR PHILADELPHIA ORCHESTRA

☆ ☆ ☆ ☆ ☆ ☆ ☆ ☆ ☆ ☆ ☆

TUES., OCT. 13 • 8:30 P.M.
ACADEMY OF MUSIC
BROAD & LOCUST STREETS

TICKETS: Academy of Music Box Office or 220 South Broad St. Philadelphia, Penna. 19102

After I had appeared with orchestras as a narrator, I made my debut as a pianist at a benefit performance with members of the Philadelphia Orchestra in 1970. Here's the poster announcing the event, at which I appeared with the tenor Jan Peerce. (Author's collection)

Arthur Fiedler and I traveled to Bonn, Germany, in 1970 to join in the celebration of the bicentennial of Beethoven's birth. During the trip I performed with Maestro Fiedler and the Boston Pops. (Helmut J. Wolf)

At a fundraiser in New York in 1970, I played the andante movement from Mozart's Piano Concerto No. 21. I had to pile one ballroom chair on another because there wasn't a proper piano bench. (The New York Times)

I had a small role to play in helping Mstislav Rostropovich defect from the Soviet Union. Here I welcome him and his wife, the soprano Galina Vishnevskaya, to my home in Washington, D.C., in 1975. (Ken Regan/Camera 5)

Sixteen years later "Slava," as he likes to be called, and I meet at a benefit concert for the New England Conservatory in Boston. (Author's collection)

the Scaffold, he takes opium and hallucinates that he has killed her and is walking to his execution.

While symphonic and solo music were developing elsewhere in Europe, in Italy, opera was still champion. Gioacchino Rossini (1792–1868) was turning them out by the yard—between the ages of eighteen and thirty he wrote thirty-two operas. Rossini's comedies are staples of opera house repertoire today. Pieces like *The Barber of Seville* (1816), which is based on the same set of French plays that Mozart plumbed for *The Marriage of Figaro,* see the world in terms of light and cheer. Melody is paramount, the singers show off their technical skill with wild flourishes, and the instrumental finales build up excitement by repeating the same idea louder and louder and faster and faster. No brooding Romanticism here—Rossini is all about beautiful singing, the "bel canto" style that was followed by other composers such as Gaetano Donizetti (1797–1848) and Vincenzo Bellini (1801–35).

Giuseppe Verdi (1813–1901) was more interested in opera as human drama, and his operas are full of strong emotions and characters. He used plays by Victor Hugo and Shakespeare as the basis for nearly a quarter of his operas, which have carefully worked out, often tragic, plots. The singing is part of the action, rather than an opportunity for technical display, but Verdi singers must have huge voices to soar over the powerful orchestrations. Verdi's canon is vast, ranging from blood-and-thunder pieces, like *Il Trovatore,* to the intimate drama about a self-sacrificing courtesan, *La Traviata,* to the tortured story of Shakespeare's hero, *Otello.* Only at the very end of his life did Verdi come up with a comedy, *Falstaff,* also based on Shakespeare.

My heart, however, belongs to Giacomo Puccini (1858–1924), who wrote operas about fragile, betrayed ladies (*La Bohème, Madama Butterfly*), giving his heroines voluptuously beautiful melodies that require lungs and vocal cords of steel. I also love *Carmen* by Georges Bizet (1838–75), which was written in 1875. Opera continued to develop in France, and *Carmen,* a bloody drama about a free-living gypsy and a smitten soldier named Don José, is full of color and Spanish spice.

Meanwhile, in Germany, an entirely new force was turning opera upside down. Richard Wagner (1813–83) had his own ideas about the lyric theater. For him, music and drama were one. None of those arias to let singers show off—Wagner had a serious agenda. Vocal parts became part of the orchestral fabric, making it easy for overenthusiastic conductors to drown them out altogether, and the music was continuous—no spectacular vocal ending, with a pause for applause. Wagner wrote his own librettos, basing them on ancient legends, not blood-and-thunder tales. *The Ring of the Nibelung,* a four-opera cycle based on Norse mythology, took Wagner twenty years to write and has gods, humans, and other unclassifiable beings as characters. It has been interpreted as signifying everything from class struggle to the decline of the West, but it is an exciting—if often long— story on its own terms. I cheat a lot with Wagner—I love to listen to the orchestral excerpts and preludes from his operas, like the swooping, crazy "Ride of the Valkyries" from *Die Walküre* and the majestic opening of *Die Meistersinger von Nürnberg,* which are gloriously lush and often dramatic.

The nineteenth-century symphonic tradition continued to unroll all over the continent. I've mentioned Tchaikovsky; Sergei Rachmaninoff (1873–1943), another favorite of mine, was a compatriot and creator of thundering symphonies and concertos with a Russian accent. The splendid Czech composer Antonín Dvořák (1841–1904) used nationalistic themes; he wrote those fiery *Slavonic Dances* that I once played in a two-piano version in Washington, some lovely wind music, and nine symphonies. One of the most famous is the ninth, called *From the New World,* which he wrote in America in 1893; it is said he used themes from American Indian music and negro spirituals in it. He also wrote a great cello concerto (which Yo-Yo also introduced me to). I'm also partial to the full-blooded symphonies of the Finn Jean Sibelius (1865–1957), especially his Symphony No. 2, which I find unbelievably erotic—it's one climax after another.

In Germany, the symphony got bigger and bigger with the massive productions of Gustav Mahler (1860–1911), who was conductor of the Vienna Opera from 1897 to 1907 and had a brief, unhappy tenure as music director of the New York Philharmonic in the last two years of his life. Richard Strauss (1864–1949) wrote symphonic poems with programs (stories), some about heroes (*Ein Heldenleben*) and others about rogues (*Till Eulenspiegel*), as well as operas. In addition to being harmonically forward-looking, some of his operas were also banned for being obscene. (*Salome* is about a not very attractive Biblical teenager who demands the head of John the Baptist in return for dancing naked for her uncle.)

In France, still other developments were occurring. Composers such as Gabriel Fauré (1845–1924) and Claude Debussy (1862–1918) reacted against the massiveness of the Germans and came up with their own innovation. Impressionism—which takes its title from the school of painting—evokes a mood, rather than telling a particular story, through washes of instrumental color in which outlines are blurred. Fauré's transcendent *Requiem,* and Debussy's shimmering orchestral picture of the sea, *La Mer,* are some of my favorite examples, plus, of course, Debussy's wonderful, limpid piano music.

In the twentieth century, things went a bit wild. Once again, the revolution started in Vienna, where Arnold

Schoenberg (1874–1951) decided that the distortions of European music's basic harmonic principles had been taken as far as they could go. His solution to the need for new forms of expression was to devise an entirely new harmonic scheme. Instead of building music around tonality—or the notes that related naturally to a particular base note, such as C, or B-flat—Schoenberg invented his own scales. He decided that any piece could use any of the twelve notes in the harmonic scale (A, A-sharp, B, C, C-sharp, and so on), and he devised principles for the arrangement and manipulation of the notes that were chosen. In Schoenberg and his followers, like Anton von Webern (1883–1945), the sounds are splintered and dissonant, yet they capture a world in which fragmentation and fear are no longer expressed symbolically—they come right to the surface. I'm fond of Webern's *Passacaglia* for orchestra with its spiky surfaces and charged silences.

Composers like Béla Bartók (1881–1945) and Igor Stravinsky (1882–1971) experimented with the twelve-tone language, yet each had his own powerful impact on the twentieth century. Bartók, a Hungarian, sought out his gypsy musical roots and passed them through the prism of the twentieth century to create a jagged, often frightening language. His six string quartets are an emotional ordeal. Stravinsky too took the Russian musical language into which he was born and transformed it into something totally modern. His *Rite of Spring,* with its twisted, pounding rhythms, is a terrifyingly primal sort of experience.

Stalinist politics almost scuttled the Russian composer Dmitri Shostakovich (1906–75), creator of fifteen symphonies and the same number of string quartets. Popular and successful, Shostakovich was broadsided in 1936 when *Pravda* attacked his opera *Lady Macbeth of the Mtzensk District,* calling it "chaos instead of music," and calling on Shostakovich and his fellows to abandon dissonant modernist idioms that were repellent to "The People." His Symphony No. 5, a favorite of mine, was written shortly after that attack, and its success reinstated him, but in 1948 he and other composers, including Sergei Prokofiev, were attacked again.

The twentieth century has been a fertile time for American composers. The most famous is Aaron Copland (1900–90), who, although he grew up in New York, became the musical voice of America's wide-open spaces. *Appalachian Spring,* the ballet he wrote for Martha Graham, and his *Fanfare for the Common Man* are two of his most famous creations, which have ensured his immortality. The eccentric Charles Ives (1874–1954) invented forms, many of which prefigured later compositional developments, but he also drew on American songs and themes. His *Variations on America,* as orchestrated by William Schuman, is a wonderfully witty kaleidoscope of a patriotic tune.

America is an amazing polyglot culture, and its composers draw from strains everywhere. During the Second World War, Schoenberg fled the Nazis and settled in southern California, perpetuating his musical theories. Bartók, too, lived here. American composers went to study in Paris with the famous pedagogue Nadia Boulanger. In the 1930s and 1940s, American symphonists like Roy Harris, William Schuman, Walter Piston, and Howard Hanson offered their own interpretations of that great Central European form. Others, however, avoided the symphony orchestra and wrote for small ensembles, sometimes devising their own instrumentations outside the traditional quartet and trio forms. Composers such as Milton Babbitt and Elliott Carter took the lessons of Schoenberg to heart and created knotty, highly intellectual music.

Others, like Leonard Bernstein (1918–90), found their inspiration closer to home. Bernstein, an extraordinary natural musician—pianist, conductor, composer, teacher, visionary—

wrote lively scores for the theater (*West Side Story* is part of our common heritage now) as well as symphonies like *Jeremiah* and *The Age of Anxiety*. As I've said before, I have a special place in my heart for his sprawling, unashamed *Mass*.

Modern composers have taken every possible direction. Some use electronic devices to write music. Others, the minimalists, have taken their cue from African drumming and reduced their music to repeated short phrases that have only tiny, incremental changes, making for a hypnotic effect. I was at a performance of the opera *Einstein on the Beach* by Philip Glass, which created a complete musical and theatrical mood—just as Wagner wished to do, but using entirely different expressive means. Today, some composers have returned to tonality, insisting that Schoenberg was wrong—the nineteenth-century composers had not reached the end of tonality's possibilities. Hundreds of composers like the Americans Ellen Taaffe Zwilich, David Del Tredici, and John Harbison, the Polish composer Witold Lutoslawski, the Englishman Oliver Knussen, the German Hans Werner Henze, and the Japanese Toru Takemitsu continue to find new ways of using this old music and making it express the feelings and ideas of the 1990s. We are in an enviable position: because our musical institutions preserve the works of centuries gone by while presenting creations of our own time, we can see how the world has changed, but also how certain things have remained the same. Mozart might not understand Philip Glass or Ellen Zwilich if he came back today, but he would certainly marvel at how those same materials that he was manipulating two centuries ago can be harnessed to the purpose of the artists of a totally different age.

SIX

Dance

W HAT IS CHRISTMASTIME without *The Nut-cracker?* It was certainly an integral part of my childhood, and of my children's. The lovely fantasy world of the first-act Christmas party, full of celebrating children, and the even more splendid second act, when little Clara, in her dream, is whirled off to a kingdom of dancing sweets, can't miss with most children. There's the plot to follow, the dancing to watch, the beautiful sets and costumes, all borne along on the glorious music of Tchaikovsky.

Tchaikovsky wrote some of his greatest music for the ballet. *Swan Lake, The Sleeping Beauty,* and *The Nutcracker* were all created for the imperial Russian court of St. Petersburg— for the Westward-looking aristocrats who loved those spectacles of dance, music, and decor. These late nineteenth-century staples are the heart of our ballet companies' repertoire today, and one of the reasons they have endured so solidly is the power of their music. You can sit and listen to those scores, and even if you had nothing to look at on the stage, you could hear exactly what was happening. The feverish, agitated theme that represents Odette, the unhappy Swan Queen heroine of *Swan Lake,* for example, speaks of tragedy and heartbreak. The exquisite violin and cello duet, to which the Prince and his bewitched queen dance their first love duet together, and the heartless, crystalline music to which the imposter Black Swan impresses the Prince's court with her feats of technical brilliance are drama in music. I once sat behind someone at the ballet who was grumbling about how all that moving around onstage was distracting him from the music!

The partnership between music and movement is what makes dance work. The great choreographer George Balanchine used to say, "See the music, hear the dance." I think it's impossible to make a good dance to bad music, and choreographers, who put the steps together to make dances, listen constantly to music to find the piece that sparks their imaginations. Some have to hear the right music before they even start to think about what sort of dance they will make, whether it's Tchaikovsky or Handel—or, these days, an Indian raga or a jazz riff. The relationship between composers and choreographers has been very dynamic in our century: Martha Graham found inspiration in the scores written for her by Aaron Copland (she commissioned his famous *Appalachian Spring*) and many others; much of Merce Cunningham's dance is defined by the revolutionary music of John Cage; George Balanchine's aesthetic vision found its mirror in the scores of Igor Stravinsky, among many others.

One of music's most basic functions, after all, is as an accompaniment to dancing. It gives the shape, the beat, the tone, and the color of what the dance will be like, whether the dance is rock and roll, salsa, a fox-trot, a Tchaikovsky ballet, or a postmodern dance to drums and synthesizers. Have you ever done any square dancing? Think about how those figures fit with the fiddling and up-tempo stomp of the music. Watch children—they will dance to anything. Think of how a waltz rhythm makes your body want to move, and how differently a syncopated beat affects you. Imagine how a sensuous melody could be reflected physically, or what kind of stage picture comes to mind when you hear a jagged, jumpy line. That's what choreographers do. And when you watch dancers onstage move to music, and mentally you start to move with them, then you're caught. Bruce Marks, the former ballet dancer who now runs the Boston Ballet, once told me, "You go to the ballet for the experience of *being* the dancer. A cool, posed performance where a dancer makes nice lines and pretty pictures is something you can admire intellectually, but until you start to feel, you can't become a ballet goer."

Choreographers work within their own vocabularies. Marius Petipa and Lev Ivanov, for example, who made those ballets at the imperial court in St. Petersburg, were doing what we now think of as classical ballet. The basic positions and movements are physically unnatural. Women dance on the points of their toes, an early nineteenth-century innovation that gave them height, speed, and the illusion of weightlessness, and made their central pose, the balance on one leg, even more spectacular. Legs are turned out from the hip, giving the dancer a full circular range of movement. Men support the women in their balances, turns, leaps, and lifts, and have their own star moments in solo sections, as they run, leap, and beat their feet together while suspended in midair. A female dancer, lifted toward the ceiling on a man's arm, or bent toward the floor, one leg raised high behind her, is the epitome of beauty and line. The fairy-tale stories of the Russian ballets and the otherworldliness of the dancers all belie the tremendous physical difficulty of executing those movements. The audience is never to see the sweat or know that those billowing, swanlike arms and necks are the fruit of rigidly disciplined training.

Today, if you attend a dance performance, you may see that traditional classical style. But the world of dance today is far broader than it was in nineteenth-century Russia. Isadora Duncan, Martha Graham, and other twentieth-century Americans shed their toe shoes and the codified movement of the ballet to create their own physical language, more of the ground than of the air, and modern dance was born. Classical ballet itself has undergone radical changes too. In 1907, the Russian choreographer Mikhail Fokine decided that ballets need not have stories, and he created a one-act plotless ballet, *Chopiniana,* later renamed *Les Sylphides,* that was a physical evocation of the music of Chopin. Then George Balanchine, first in Paris and then in New York, carried that traditional language to new extremes of speed, flexibility, rhythmic complexity, visual patterns, and abstract content. Too poor to afford the lavish costumes and the decor of his native Russian ballet, he made a virtue of necessity and put his dancers onstage in the tights and leotards of the classroom and rehearsal studio. His innovation became a trend, and when these stripped-down dancers perform, the audience sees pure movement.

Dance today is more than fairy stories. The murderous impulses, thwarted passions, and desperate loves that were played out in symbolic ways in the classical tradition get more down-to-earth treatment from modern dancers. Childbirth, murder, and vampirism may turn up in full view. Or there may be no story at all. Dance steps are combined, but the patterns they create may not have any particular narrative story to tell.

The dance scene is extraordinarily diverse. Modern dancers have split away from Martha Graham's pioneering language to create their own. Paul Taylor's is physical, almost balletic in its lift and speed; Alvin Ailey's is rooted in African-American dance; Mark Morris's seems to have taken something from everyone. Modern dancer-choreographers usually have their own companies, which play a few weeks in their home city (usually New York) and spend as much of the rest of the year as possible touring at home and abroad.

Some of today's ballet companies are, like the modern dance companies, laboratories for a single choreographic mind—Balanchine's New York City Ballet, for example, or Eliot Feld's company. Other companies pursue a more eclectic range of styles, inviting choreographers to create new works, and reviving old ones from many different choreographic schools. Some have cross-fertilized, inviting modern dance choreographers to make dances for their ballet dancers. The result is an exciting mix of styles. A company may show *Swan Lake* one night, and a double bill of Balanchine and Paul Taylor the next. Ballet dancers have experimented with other styles as well: the celebrated ballet dancer Mikhail Baryshnikov performed with Martha Graham's company and has recently collaborated with Mark Morris, a current young sensation.

Today's ballet dancers need to be as versatile as the symphony musicians are, seamlessly switching gears from sensuous Romantic expression to fleet, craggy modernism within a single performance. Gender distinctions may be much less emphasized, too, especially in modern dance, where women may support other women in lifts and turns, and everyone is often garbed in the same, unisex costume. Just as the thundering scores of Tchaikovsky are different from the dissonances of Prokofiev and Elliott Carter, so too does the frail, ethereal ballerina supported by the virile male dancer reflect an earlier age.

I did some ballet going when I was a child, and I took my children to special events in Washington, but I got my real indoctrination into ballet when I moved to Boston in the 1980s. At the time, my friend Mary Ellen Cabot was chairman of the Boston Ballet board. She was always looking for friends to sit in her box, and I was almost always willing. At the time, the company was run by Violette Verdy, who had been a ballerina with Balanchine in the New York City Ballet. Now Bruce Marks, who was a principal dancer with American Ballet Theatre and the Royal Danish Ballet, heads it. The company has forty-six dancers and an extremely varied repertoire.

I got turned on to the athleticism of dance. I guess I'm an exception to the cult of the ballerina (even Balanchine the revolutionary still believed that "ballet is a woman"), in that I'm especially thrilled by male dancers. Their incredible strength and agility is breathtaking. My son Teddy, who occasionally went to the ballet with me in Boston, was hooked in the same way. Teddy, after all, is a great sports enthusiast, and he was stunned by the things that these dancers could do with their incredibly trained and disciplined bodies. Teddy prefers modern ballet to the nineteenth-century story ballets —but he's open-minded about it. Our dance going prompted one of those calls that every mother longs to get from her college-age son: he was dating a former ballerina, and he called to ask me what performance he should take her to, and what he should know about it beforehand!

Those years at the Boston Ballet also showed me that there is more to dance than my beloved *Nutcracker*—and more than dancing on toe. The range of styles that most modern ballet companies encompass is almost bewildering. I love the variety of mixed-program evenings. When the curtain goes up, you're never sure what you'll see. It might be the thrilling athleticism of Paul Taylor's *Esplanade,* in which the dancers' bodies simply hurtle through the air, or the shifting patterns of Balanchine's classic *Symphony in C,* to the music of Bizet. Or there might be Jerome Robbins' practice-room duet, *Afternoon of a Faun,* to Debussy's ethereal flute music, followed by Kenneth MacMillan's *Concerto* to Shostakovich, all angles and edges, and finishing up with Agnes de Mille's ebullient and utterly American *Rodeo,* to a score by Aaron Copland. Jerome Robbins' playful *Fancy Free,* to the music of Leonard Bernstein, and his serene Chopin "piano ballet" *Dances at a Gathering* show two sides of his personality, while the delicacy and graciousness of Frederick Ashton's *Les Patineurs* or the wit of his *La Fille Mal Gardée* demonstrate the aesthetic that shaped English ballet in the last sixty years. The utterly classical *Les Sylphides,* with the full corps de ballet of women in their knee-length, floating skirts of white tulle, might be followed by Baryshnikov cutting loose in *Nine Sinatra Songs,* a reinterpretation of American ballroom dancing by Twyla Tharp (a modern dance choreographer).

Those Sinatra songs really strike a resonant chord with me —not surprisingly, given my own background in dance. I never took ballet lessons or went through an adolescent fixation on ballet. My early dance training, like that of so many Westchester girls of my era, was ballroom dancing lessons at the local dancing school. The girls (in white gloves) and boys lined up together, and the pianist pounded out fox-trots, rumbas, and especially waltzes. I loved it. I still love it. I'll take any excuse for dancing. I'll never forget the day Teddy came home from a party and said, "You know what, Mom? There's a great new dance craze now—touch dancing!" Fred Astaire's movies were the height of romance for me. I watch them and imagine myself gliding around the ballroom in his arms. That—rather than dancing with Baryshnikov, much as I admire him—is still my fantasy.

Social dancing is really all of a piece with classical dancing. In fact, ballet grew out of the social dances of the courts of the Renaissance. Sixteenth-century Italian noblemen put on performances for themselves and distinguished visitors; the dancers were amateurs, the patterns and steps devised by ballet masters. In midcentury, a royal marriage between Catherine de Médicis and Henry II brought the art to France, where it flourished. New French social dances—the gavotte, galliard, rigadoon, minuet—were assimilated into these ever more complex spectacles. (If you look at the names of movements of pieces from this period, you'll see these dance names. When an orchestra plays a Haydn minuet, it should sound as though a roomful of ladies and gentlemen are dancing.)

Under Louis XIV, who reigned from 1643 until 1715 and was an enthusiastic dancer himself, the French dance grew ever more popular, sophisticated, and professionalized. Soon it was incorporated into the opera, and a whole new form, the opera-ballet—made up of dancing, singing, and lavish decor, with Greek or Roman mythical tales as themes—grew up in France under the direct patronage of the crown. The French court composers Lully and Rameau created their greatest works for these spectacles. Ballet made its way to the imperial court at Vienna as well, and from there to Russia.

Eighteenth-century ballet was much different from today's, however. The women, wearing skirts just short enough to display their ankles, wore heeled shoes and used very circumscribed movements. Extremely expressive gestures of the neck, shoulders, arms, and hands communicated emotion. It took a century or so for women to put on the toe shoes that are the hallmark of classical ballet today, increase turnout of the legs to 180 degrees, raise their skirts into the now traditional ruff around the hips, the tutu, to expose the full line of their legs, and start making the lofty leaps that were once exclusively the province of male dancers.

The nineteenth century saw the flowering of Romantic ballet. Romanticism—the hero's search for his soul, the mystical qualities of nature, as embodied in novels by Sir Walter Scott and others—seemed tailor-made for the ballet. In 1832, the choreographer Filippo Taglioni created the ballet *La Sylphide* for his daughter Marie. Light and otherworldly in a diaphanous skirt and that brand-new innovation, pointe shoes, Marie Taglioni played the Scottish woodland fairy who entices practical James away from his down-to-earth family and fiancée—with disastrous consequences. After Taglioni's success, dancing on toe became de rigueur. Ten years later, Jules Perrot created another Romantic staple, *Giselle,* for his favorite pupil, Carlotta Grisi. *Giselle* is also about women who lure men to their deaths: the peasant girl Giselle, betrayed by a prince posing as a commoner, goes mad and dies. She becomes a Wili, one of a ghostly tribe of girls who have died unmarried, and who make unsuspecting men dance themselves to death. Romance being what it is, Giselle of course saves her now repentant prince from his fate.

In Denmark, August Bournonville (1805–79) made his contribution to Romantic ballet with his own version of *La Sylphide* (it has survived; Taglioni's has not) and a style of dance that featured buoyant, joyous peasants rather than aristocrats and created a Danish ballet tradition that is still going strong today.

Romantic ballet had only a brief vogue in Europe, but its practitioners found new and fertile ground in Russia. By the century's end, Marius Petipa, French by birth, and his collaborator and successor, Lev Ivanov, were concocting elaborate dance spectacles in St. Petersburg. The great Russian composers of the day wrote splendid scores based on legends and fairy tales, such as *Swan Lake* (Petipa's version: 1895). The bewitched Swan Queen, the Prince, the evil magician, and the corps de ballet of swans work out their fates in three dramatic acts, all wrapped up in the sweeping music of Tchaikovsky. The plot is spelled out in explicit gestures and musical statements, the physical characteristics of the swans clearly specified in movement, while the love duets, the divertissements (court, folk, or exotic dances that round out the action), and the final apotheosis of the doomed lovers are all built into a grand, symphonic design.

Then Serge Diaghilev, the Russian impresario, changed the face of ballet altogether. He took his Ballet Russe to Paris in 1909, with the intention of presenting the best of Russian art to the West, and revitalized the art form. He brought the ballets of Fokine and championed his own choreographers, bringing them together with artists like Picasso and Matisse, and composers such as Stravinsky, Erik Satie, Maurice Ravel, Sergei Prokofiev, and Francis Poulenc, to create entirely new kinds of ballet. He commissioned *Rite of Spring* from Stravinsky and gave it to his principal dancer, Vaslav Nijinsky, to choreograph. The 1913 premiere in Paris was a scandal: the savage musical rhythms and explicit choreography (the ballet was about fertility and human sacrifice) horrified the Paris public, which liked its exoticism a bit more colorful and remote.

When Diaghilev died in 1929, his artists went on. Ida Rubinstein, one of his choreographers, was responsible for Maurice Ravel's now famous *Boléro*. Marie Rambert—a disciple of the music-movement pioneer Dalcroze who was brought in to help the musically illiterate Nijinsky translate his ideas to the dancers in *Rite of Spring*—went back to England to found a school and produce a whole generation of English dancers. Ninette de Valois, who had also performed with the Ballet Russe, founded what is today the Royal Ballet.

George Balanchine (1904–83) joined Diaghilev in 1924. He created his *Apollon Musagète* (1928) with Stravinsky and *Prodigal Son* (1929) with Prokofiev under Diaghilev's umbrella. Discovered by a wealthy American dance enthusiast in Paris in 1933, he went to the United States, which was then pretty much without any classical dance traditions. He founded first a school, and then ultimately the New York City Ballet, and imposed his own aesthetic on a whole country of ballet companies.

The United States was a fertile ground for dance. New York became home to several companies: not only the New York City Ballet, but also American Ballet Theatre, founded in 1940, flourished there. Ballet Theatre, which performed the classics, also nourished such choreographers as Antony Tudor (1909–87). Tudor's ballets, such as *Lilac Garden* (a wrenching quartet about missed opportunities in love, to the music of Ernest Chausson), *Pillar of Fire* (about a woman's sexual frustration and fear, to a score by Arnold Schoenberg), and *Undertow* (about a woman-hating murderer, to music by William Schuman), used the powerfully expressionistic sentiments of modern dance in a classical ballet vocabulary.

Ballet companies sprang up outside New York as well. In 1938, Willam Christensen took over the fledgling San Francisco Ballet. He started the American tradition of *The Nutcracker* at Christmas with his 1944 staging. Alumni from the New York City Ballet have started companies all over the country; one of the most unusual, Arthur Mitchell's outstanding Dance Theater of Harlem, was started in 1969 as a way to both get poor black children off the streets and showcase black talent in classical dance.

Dance—both classical and modern—remains one of the most exciting and innovative of the performing arts. Unlike

music audiences, who often prefer to hear the same composers and pieces played over and over again, dance audiences—
like theatergoers—love novelty and creativity. They look forward eagerly to their favorite choreographer's newest work,
and they debate it enthusiastically. When "New Ballet" appears on the season's schedule, it is cause for anticipation.

Most major American cities have ballet companies today;
many have modern dance troupes. Companies are fed by
local and company schools. Ballet schools may enroll very
young children in "preballet" movement classes, much like
early childhood music classes, which are designed to stimu-
late and encourage the child's innate capacity for movement
and musicality. Starting at age seven or eight, children may
start the basic work of classical training, a study that lasts ten
years and more. Ballet dancers must begin young: their flexible bodies can more easily be molded into the turned-out
positions that are basically unnatural. In these beginning
classes, children learn the five basic positions of the feet and
arms, and the first simple movements used to pass from one
to the next, which is what choreography is all about. They
learn the French terms for them: since ballet grew up in
France, it was disseminated in that language. Like the Italian
musical terms, the French words are absolutely descriptive.
Take *fouetté,* for example, a movement in which the dancer
turns on one leg, while the other is raised ninety degrees to
the side, and the lower half of the working leg whips around
in a semicircle. The word means "whip." (The Black Swan
of *Swan Lake*'s Act III does thirty-two of these in a row—a
tour de force of balance and skill.) *Pas de chat* (cat step) is a
step in which the feet leave the floor in quick, furtive succes-
sion—like a cat's.

Students begin classes holding on to a bar, where they
learn correct position, and then move into the center of the

room, where they do combinations and jumps. Toe work should not start before the child is twelve, in order not to damage growing feet. Children begin with one class a week, building up to one a day or sometimes more for those who are serious. Children at company-affiliated schools, like the School of American Ballet at the New York City Ballet, are bent on professional careers, so the training of their bodies tends to take precedence over all other activities. Some talented young people may find themselves in ballet companies when they are fifteen or sixteen, dancing in the corps de ballet, and then possibly advancing to small solo and finally leading roles.

Given its physical demands, ballet is a young person's art. Injuries and strain take their toll, usually forcing dancers to retire, or at least curtail their activities, by the time they are forty. There are exceptions, of course. The great ballerina Margot Fonteyn was over forty when she began her legendary partnership with the thrilling Russian defector Rudolf Nureyev. Nureyev, now in his midfifties, is still dancing. I met Fonteyn and Nureyev at the White House soon after they began their partnership in 1962, the year after he defected. She was a charmer; he was incredibly sexy, with his Tatar eyes, and spoke barely a word of English. Watching the two together onstage—the flower-like, English ballerina and the savage Russian—was electric.

Modern dancers tend to start later and go on longer—Merce Cunningham is still dancing, and he is over seventy. College dance departments have become a prime training ground for these dancers, who then join the companies of particular choreographers and become steeped in their aesthetics.

If you're going to attend a dance performance for the first time, examine the options in town and nearby. If the local college or university has a dance department, this may be a good (and inexpensive) first experience. There may be a professional ballet company, and local concert hall or university presenters of outside events bring in a lot of dance of various kinds—not only Western classical and modern, but drum and dance troupes from Africa, shadow plays from Indonesia, and folk-dance groups from Russia and Eastern Europe, which provide a fascinating contrast. To get more information even before you buy your tickets, check out lectures and demonstrations. The Boston Ballet now gives many preperformance lectures and does different outreach programs; you might want to investigate similar offerings in your community.

To start, you might try a full-evening story ballet, like *Swan Lake* or *Coppélia* (a delightful romp to the music of Léo Delibes about a boy who falls for a life-sized doll, and how his girlfriend punishes him for straying). You could also attend a mixed program of modern and classical ballet, or an evening with the work of a single modern dance choreographer's company. Try to find out the music that the choreographers have used (often it is listed in the advance brochure) to see if it is something with which you are familiar. Your preferences in visual art may give you clues about what sort of dance to try. If you enjoy abstract painting, you might like some of the modern dance choreographers best; if your taste runs to narrative, try a story ballet. *The Nutcracker,* a holiday money-maker for most ballet companies, is a delightful beginning for children. (When Teddy Jr. was small, he used to enjoy listening to excerpts from *The Nutcracker* at home.) But don't stop there. Just as children may be more receptive to cacophonous modern sounds that take adults a lot of time to adjust to, your budding balletomane may also see the excitement of dance without tutus and toe shoes.

SEVEN

Music at Home

WHEN I HAD a family of my own, I wanted music to be a part of all our lives, so I did the same thing my mother did—I had it playing all the time. The single, massive radio in the front hall of the forties and fifties gave way to record players and speakers in every room—and mountains of tapes, records, and now compact discs—as I, and later my children, explored repertoire. It wasn't just for the kids, of course. I was playing music for my own pleasure, and even now that all three are grown and no longer live with me, I still have music on almost constantly.

Kara, Teddy Jr., and Patrick got used to that music. They heard it constantly. Their earliest memories are bound up with music—either me playing the piano, or recorded music resounding through the house—so there was nothing strange about it to them. When my children's friends visited and asked what was on the radio or the record player, the response was always "Oh, that's my mother's music" and "No, we don't turn it off." My kids thought classical music was perfectly normal, and they grew to like it. They certainly never objected to it.

That's why I think that music should become part of life for parents if they want their children to enjoy it. Kids know when you're putting one over on them—when you're giving them something because you think it's "good for them," as opposed to something you really believe in for yourself. Also, if you start early, and music is part of daily life while your young children are exploring their world, they will accept it as they accept any other element in your household. They may rebel later and want to introduce you to other kinds of music—I'm all for that, too—but this way they'll have a solid foundation that will always be there.

The first step, then, is to build your own familiarity with classical music. You can get started on your explorations without specialized knowledge or expense. For a very basic guide to the composers and periods of music, look at Chapter Five and the Appendix of this book, but your own ears, and your own tastes, ultimately will determine the sort of music you listen to.

Find the classical radio station in your area—most major markets have at least one—and listen to it for a few days. Leave it on in the house and in the car. Notice which pieces you like, listen for their titles and composers, and note them down if you have the opportunity. Listen for different kinds of music—the big orchestral sound, the sparer effect of chamber music (which has just a few instruments), the solo violin, cello, oboe, or flute with piano, the piano alone, the voice with piano or orchestra, opera, or the wonderful massed voices of a chorus.

Next, investigate the public library. Most lend records. Choose a few; you can base your selections on your radio listening, composers or pieces you might have heard of, or suggestions from Chapter Five—or just pick at random. Browse a bit: maybe you've always liked the sound of the flute, or wondered what a harpsichord was like, or wanted to know why Beethoven is famous. Don't worry about which performer to choose, unless you'd like to listen to a recording by someone whose name you recognize and whom you've been curious about.

When you've chosen, take the records home and play them to death for a week. Get to know them so that their language is second nature to you. Soon you'll be recognizing their shapes and melodies, anticipating their climaxes and their slow and fast sections, playing along with their tension and release. Then take the records back and get a few more. Try more music by the same composers—perhaps chamber or solo music this time if you chose orchestral before—or pick out some different ones. Repeat the process several times. The music of a particular period, such as Baroque, Classical, or Romantic, which I describe in Chapter Five, may appeal to you, or you might want to listen to something by a twentieth-century composer. It's not necessary to like everything. Some music is an acquired taste, but if you give it a chance, you may be surprised at what appeals to you. Perhaps the sweeping melodies of the symphonies of Tchaikovsky will turn out to be your preference, or the spiky, anguished moods of the Bartók string quartets, the elegant, poetic songs of Schubert, the urgent supplication of the chorus in Bach's *St. Matthew Passion,* or the slow changes and hypnotic rhythms of *Different Trains,* an unusual work for string quartet woven through with spoken words, by the contemporary composer Steve Reich.

You needn't sit down and listen to the pieces all the way

through at first, unless you feel like it. Play them as background music for a while, just to get their sound into your ear—in the morning when you're getting dressed, for example, or while you're cooking. In my family, just as in my childhood, music was always an important part of mealtime, especially dinner. Ted always made a special effort to be home for dinner with us, even if he had to go back to his office later, so we made the meal an event: we ate in the dining room, and there was always music on.

I've always found music wonderful for relaxation. After dinner, when the children were in bed or in their rooms, Ted and I would sometimes sit in our den with the fire going. He'd plow through briefcases full of papers in preparation for a committee meeting or the introduction of a bill; I'd read, and we'd have something like Rimsky-Korsakov's colorful Russian fantasy *Scheherazade* or Respighi's beautiful Italian landscape in sound, *The Pines of Rome,* playing. I almost always chose something pictorial for that time of day. It was soothing, and it helped us unwind and think, even subliminally, of something other than the pressures and tensions of the day.

Eventually, you will want to start paying attention to the pieces you listen to—you will find that they demand it. Soon your preferences for certain composers and certain kinds of music will start to develop, and you will want to start buying your own records, tapes, and compact discs. I like to make tapes of my favorite pieces or sections of pieces for the car or the beach. There are times of the day when I just want to listen to a lot of slow music, so I'll pick out the slow movements of concertos or symphonies and play them back to back.

There are other avenues for finding out more about classical music. Many adult education programs offer music courses; if you want more information, and you're the sort of person who learns best in a class situation, that may be useful. In the just-for-fun department, go to see—or rent—some movies with stories about classical musicians. A recent gem, *Impromptu,* is a wild story about the beginning of the famous love affair between the composer Chopin and the novelist George Sand. The music is cleverly worked in: in one scene, Chopin gives the lovesick Sand one minute to make her pitch to him—and plays the "Minute" waltz as she does it. Other members of their artistic circle (which flourished in Paris in the 1830s), such as Franz Liszt and Alfred de Musset, also appear. The movie biography of Mozart, *Amadeus,* is now a classic, and deservedly so; the music, stunningly performed, is as brilliant and vital an element as the acting and cinematography. *Diva,* a cult classic, features a glamorous opera singer, and *Meeting Venus* is also about the exotic operatic world. *The Competition* is a love story built around a piano competition; *Madame Sousatzka* explores the highly charged relationship between a piano teacher and her gifted pupil. Among the oldies, *Fantasia,* the cartoon version of some of the classics of the repertoire, is evergreen, and some of the hoary old composer biographies (*A Song to Remember,* also about Chopin, for example) are fun, if a bit overwrought at times.

Once music becomes a part of your home life, you will start to see your children respond to it. It soothes cranky babies—there are actual studies that chart the reactions of infants to different kinds of music. They can dance to it—or you can dance them, if they are infants—and even tiny babies will sing along. Music is also wonderful for nap time. When I was student teaching as part of my master's degree requirement, I found that children were glad to lie down on the floor and rest if I put some beautiful music on. Of course,

I always used to give a prize to the quietest child, which probably had something to do with their docility.

Creating an atmosphere in which music is a vital component is really the goal here. Classical music was the basic currency in our house because I loved it, but the operetta and Broadway musical songs that my mother sang were just as important as the symphonies I heard on the radio in fostering my love of music. If you enjoy popular music or jazz, you should play that too. Just as in a house without books children don't learn to value words and reading, in a house without music they don't recognize it as being a means of expression and communication that has something to do with them.

Music is a personal art, one that *people* do. A young child cannot grasp that fact merely by listening to recordings, because while the child may hear the music, he has no visual reference for it. Thus, live performance is an important facet of early musical introduction. Since taking infants and very young children to concerts isn't usually an option, live performance means you.

I played the piano for my kids. I was busy, certainly—the politician's wife is always on the run—but I always found some time, somewhere, to practice the piano, and I tried to do it when Kara, Teddy, and Patrick were around. They still remember creeping quietly into the living room to sit on the sofa and listen. It might have been for just a few minutes, but they got the idea that music was important to me, that it was something I did. Rose Kennedy, my mother-in-law, played a lot too, so the kids got used to hearing her play, and the two of us playing piano four-hands. My kids were always proud of my playing, too, and that made me feel good. Parents are the most important figures in the lives of little children, and they want to do what their parents do.

You needn't be a trained instrumentalist to make music

for and with your child. Any instrument will work, and any kind of music. If you play guitar, harmonica, or double bass, sing opera arias or "Pop Goes the Weasel," you make the point. If you really can't manage any kind of "performing," listen to records and tapes *with* your child.

The one thing that nearly everyone can do, however, is sing. Start singing to your child from birth. You may think you have a voice like a frog, or one like the opera star Luciano Pavarotti, but babies are not critics, and they'll love whatever you do. Even if you think you can't sing at all, even if you were made to stand in the back of the chorus and mouth the words when you were in school, don't be put off. Very few people are truly tone-deaf and really can't carry a tune at all. If you're unsure, try singing along with some records of children's songs—you'll see how quickly you pick up the knack. And watching the baby respond to the tones, the movement of your voice, and the sound of the words makes it all worthwhile. Lullabies and baby-bouncing songs have been part of a parent's arsenal from the beginning of time, so don't neglect them! Learn all you can. You'll soon find yourself making up your own songs for your infant, using rhythm and melody and setting words, the baby's name, or just nonsense syllables to notes—just like a composer.

I'm all for reading to children from a very early age too, and one nice way to combine music and reading is by choosing books that illustrate songs. Nursery rhyme collections are one obvious choice, and handsomely illustrated editions exist for all sorts of songs, such as "The Fox Went Out on a Chilly Night" and "Frog Went A-Courting." Pictures add a new dimension, and when they have pictures available, preverbal children can indicate exactly which song they'd like to hear.

Many records of children's songs exist. When my kids were small, Pete Seeger was popular, and his tapes are still available and wonderful. Today, one of the best artists for children is the Canadian singer Raffi, who has released numerous audiotapes and two excellent concert videos. Raffi—who performs either on his own, playing guitar, or with a small band—sings very directly, without affectation, and many of his songs invite some sort of audience participation. His videos have no fancy effects or camerawork; they are concerts which show performers and the audience of children and parents having a wonderful time. Small children adore him. I know a little girl who, from the age of about a year, was positively obsessed with Raffi. She wanted to see his picture—and draw it herself. She gave the picture gifts and insisted that it be read stories. As far as she was concerned, the letter "R" stood for Raffi. As she got older, she would watch his concert tapes with increasing concentration, dancing and performing all the participation games along with the children in the audience. Still under two, she started singing his songs and asking to have them played at the piano. Small children often pick out familiar figures to admire and emulate, and I think that a wonderful musical performer is a splendid choice. Who knows—if it's Raffi today, it may well be a great violinist or opera singer when they're older.

If you watch and listen to the tapes too, it gives the activity added value for the child. (That's another advantage of Raffi —he's so good that even adults can enjoy endless hearings of "Baby Beluga" and "Morningtown Ride.") You can point out things in the music and on the video—identifying the sound of the guitar or other instrument, for example—or just enjoy the music together. And if you listen to the tapes, you learn the songs (the words are usually included in the package), so when the child asks you to sing them, you can oblige. Many performers also put out songbooks (Raffi has several) so that the fledgling piano player or guitarist parent can accompany his or her performance.

Music is not just a spectator sport, so I think it is essential that children begin doing just as soon as they can. Bouncing, jumping, and swaying to music is a fine way to begin, and singing is really the most basic musical activity of all. Little children love to sing, starting with warbling infant vocalises and renditions of favorite songs with nonspecific tunes. When the child finally puts all the elements together into actual singing, it's miraculous. I think it's a shame that people get self-conscious about their singing so quickly, considering what a joy it is, and how easily accessible. So encourage your children to sing, and sing with them. If your child has a birthday party, get a college student with a guitar to lead singing for half an hour—or do it yourself, if you can. Singing is a great thing for families to do together, too. Mine always liked rounds (like "Row, Row, Row Your Boat"), which certainly came in handy for diverting the kids when they were sick of being cooped up on long car trips. To sing a round properly, you really have to pay attention or you won't come in at the right place, and paying attention is a great way for a child to forget about incipient claustrophobia.

Singing was always an important part of Kennedy family gatherings. We used to write new lyrics to popular songs to celebrate birthdays; everyone would get a song sheet and be expected to join in. Christmas carol sings were always a big tradition, and every Labor Day was a command performance at Hyannis Port: the whole clan would gather, Rose or I or both of us would play, and everyone would sing for hours—kids, teenagers, adults, grandparents. One of those gatherings stands out in my mind: I was playing the piano and Jack Kennedy, who was then President, was singing. Jack had a lot of enthusiasm, but not a great sense of pitch. He kept wandering from key to key, so I had to keep transposing to keep up with him!

Such family sing-alongs certainly made an impression on my son Patrick. He studied singing in college, and at a fund-raising clambake for his Rhode Island House of Representatives election one summer, he took the microphone and started leading everyone in everything from "America the Beautiful" and "God Bless America" to Irish ditties, favorites of the Kennedy and Fitzgerald families. It was such a success that he's made it a regular feature of these sorts of events.

Musical toys and instruments are also a wonderful way to encourage a child's exploration. A colorful music box makes a great baby gift. Some music boxes are also designed so that the baby can operate them easily by pulling a string or pushing a button. Stuffed animals that play music are comforting friends in the crib, and musical mobiles are lovely to watch and listen to.

For a toddler who wants to pick things up, shake them, bang them, and see how they work, musical instruments are ideal. Tinkling rattles give way to maracas, tambourines, bells, and drums. Xylophones with brightly colored keys and mallets are appealing, as are toy pianos. Some of the toy keyboard instruments (which can be bought for under twenty dollars) include song cards written in standard notation, with the musical notes colored to match the appropriate keys on the instrument. This way the parent (and ultimately, the child) can actually play recognizable tunes on the instrument. Chicco makes a good xylophone-piano combination with nice large piano keys and song cards. Even if the child isn't ready to play tunes, she can bang away at the keys and start to understand for herself the physical concepts of low notes and high notes, loud and soft, scales, and the like.

Songbooks with color-coded keyboards and microchip-produced notes work the same way, though the sound quality and physical sensation are not as satisfying as those of an instrument. Still, they are good for children at many different age and ability levels—and they're terrific for car trips. The youngest children may just like to look at the pictures and have you sing and play the songs for them. My four-year-old godson, who has a book like this, can play some of the simpler tunes himself now, and whenever I visit, he runs to get it so that we can play and sing together.

Blown instruments are also fun. Anybody can get a sound out of a harmonica just by breathing in and out, and plastic recorders are wonderful beginning instruments. Catalogues such as "Music for Little People" (Box 1460, Redway, CA 95560; 1-800-346-4445) are a good source for some of these, as well as for more sophisticated instruments, including exotic African talking drums, Indian flutes, and Peruvian panpipes.

As with the singing, the great thing is for the adult to participate. Watch and admire; demonstrate a next step. Have a family songfest. Play guitar and sing, get someone else to play harmonica, and ask the child to play the tambourine, maracas, or drums. It doesn't have to be Carnegie Hall material; the point is to have fun with music.

By using simple children's songs and the child's pleasure in exploration and participation, as well as by playing classical music in the house, you set the stage for an early interest in classical music. Classical music becomes just another style of putting sounds together, an activity that the child has enjoyed with the simpler forms. There are numerous ways to involve the young child in specifically classical music.

Real instruments are one way. They are beautiful to look at, and they have strange shapes and intriguing sounds. Even very young children can benefit from having the chance to touch and play around with them. If you have a piano in your house, let the child climb up on the bench and bang away at the keys. Let him strum the guitar while you change the chords. If you have friends who play, ask them to bring their instruments over, and let the child feel the air coming out of the trumpet, or try to make a sound by drawing a bow across a violin string. If outdoor concerts are available in your town, take your child to one and bring him up close to the stage to look at the musicians and instruments. If you don't have immediate access to instruments, try the local museum. It may have a collection that you can at least look at.

Pictures of instruments are the next best thing. Children love to learn the names of things, so why not add "flute" and "violin" to their vocabularies? I've seen plastic table mats with labeled pictures of whole families of instruments. I'm also captivated by a book called *Musical Max* (text by Robert Kraus, pictures by Jose Aruego and Ariane Dewey, published by Simon & Schuster), the tale of a little hippopotamus who plays all sorts of instruments, much to the consternation of his father (though not his mother) and his neighbors, until he decides one day that he's no longer in the mood for music, and they discover how much they miss it. *Musical Max* has pictures of all kinds of instruments—with Max playing them. Even children under two love to pick out the instruments in the pictures, and they will avidly follow the story.

Of course, what's missing in books is the sound of the instruments, so you have to provide the sound effects yourself or start pointing out "flute" and "violin" for the child when you hear it on recordings. Concert videotapes can be very useful for this purpose as well: as the camera zooms in on a player, the child can hear and see the oboe or big double bass, and as it pulls back, she can see the whole ensemble, with conductor. Don't underestimate the visual impact of an orchestra, either: William Schuman, a famous American composer and a 1989 Kennedy Center honoree, got interested in composition when he attended his first concert at the age of nineteen and was fascinated by all those violinists drawing their bows across the strings of their instruments in unison.

Which brings us to the issue of television. Many parents worry about the effects of too much television on their children, and certainly there's nothing worse than seeing your child stare vacantly at the screen for hours. But I believe that television has tremendous potential for teaching, if it is used properly. In specifically child-oriented programs, classical music turns up occasionally. "Sesame Street" has been particularly good at this. One of the most hilarious spots on one of the programs features Seiji Ozawa, the renowned Japanese conductor of the Boston Symphony, leading the All-Animal Orchestra and the tenor Placido Flamingo (who is, of course, a flamingo) in an operetta aria. Each animal makes a small range of noises, which are put together into an orchestrated melody that accompanies the vocal flights of the vain but very talented Placido. Ozawa, introduced at the start as "that great good sport," never says a word: he conducts, bows, smiles, shakes hands—beaks?—with the soloist, and exits.

Ozawa is not the only classical artist to visit "Sesame Street." The Irish flutist James Galway has been on, and the violinist Isaac Stern does a sort of Pied Piper number, leading a procession of small children—and Big Bird—around the set as he plays the catchy and very funny march from Prokofiev's opera *Love for Three Oranges*.

Classical music also shows up on regular commercial television, though not quite as directly. As the music's language becomes more familiar to you, you will start to notice it in television commercials. Why not teach children to listen for it? With the visuals to hold their attention, older kids can focus on the music and how it works. The trick is to make them aware of how much of the impact is coming from the music, to make them notice the music and not take it for granted, to help them bring it out of the background and into the foreground.

Music, you will find, adds a vital dimension to movies and television. I used to tell my kids to close their eyes while we were watching and figure out, from the music, what was happening. They got to be pretty good: they always knew when the villain was coming, or if the lovers were going to kiss. You can play that game with any soundtrack, whether it uses famous music—like the gorgeous Puccini arias, sung by Kiri Te Kanawa, in *A Room with a View,* and the Strauss in *2001* —or music written especially for the movie, such as the film scores John Williams composes. (You can often find recordings of soundtracks to enjoy after the movie is over.) Learning the principles of drama in music from music that is attached to pictures can help children imagine their own associations for music when there are no pictures.

Classical music can also be worked into other home activities. When my kids played musical chairs at their birthday parties, I used classical music to start and stop them as they circled the chairs. For small kids, little dime store musical instruments, like plastic harmonicas, horns, and recorders, make good party favors. They also make great Christmas stocking stuffers. For older kids and teenagers, board games like Parker Brothers Encore and Music Maestro II are fun and terrific for learning about composers and music. If you can't or don't want to buy a lot of toys yourself, offer them as suggestions when a friend or grandparent asks what gift would be good for the child's birthday.

Another wonderful way to expose children to music is through books. I mentioned *Musical Max;* there are many others that have some musical component that are appropriate for children at all age levels. Storybooks that feature mu-

sic as an integral or peripheral part of the story show children that music is a natural part of life. The beautiful picture
book *Voice of the Wood* is the tale of an instrument maker in
Venice who creates a cello that reflects the character of the
person who plays it. Scott Gustafson's *Animal Orchestra* is a
wonderfully illustrated counting book. *I Like the Music* (ages
four to eight) is about a little girl who doesn't like classical
music until she goes to a concert in a park. An amusing tale
for the four-to-eight group is *Mama Don't Allow,* about a
child who sneaks off to play the saxophone for an alligator
party—with predictable results. *Pet of the Met* tells the story
of a mouse who lives at the Metropolitan Opera.

Some composers' life stories appeal particularly to kids.
Mozart was a child prodigy, for example, traveling and performing all over Europe during most of his childhood; Bach
had more than twenty children; Beethoven, totally deaf when
he composed his last works, conducted the premiere of his
Ninth Symphony and had to be turned toward the audience
to see their applause. Children respond to genius, to the idea
of someone sitting down and improvising a symphony at the
piano, as well as to creators who struggle on their own, doing
things that no one else really understands. On the informa-
tional side, *Music* by Neil Ardley, part of the Eyewitness
series, is an interesting historical and technical view of music
that older children will enjoy. It is full of information—a
description of how a violin is made, for example—and has
good photographs of instruments from around the world,
including rock guitars. Nicely illustrated children's songbooks are great, too. Some even have instructions for singing
games.

Illustrated books that tell the stories of operas or ballets
are also fascinating. You can read aloud the story of Mozart's
The Magic Flute, for instance (there is a beautiful version by
Margaret Greaves with jewel-like illustrations by Francesca

Crespi), or Tchaikovsky's ballets *The Nutcracker, Swan Lake,* or *Sleeping Beauty,* and then play some of the music.

Books for older children include Cynthia Voigt's *Dicey's Song,* about a girl whose singing and piano playing get her through a difficult time; *Fingers,* by William Sleator, about a fifteen-year-old prodigy possessed by the spirit of a composer; and the perennial favorite, *The Cricket in Times Square,* by George Selden, about a cricket who plays classical music on his legs for commuters. Noel Streatfeild's *Ballet Shoes* is a wonderful story about three adopted girls and their lives in dance.

Records are, of course, the most direct way for children to find out about music, and they enjoy listening to them, especially when the records are their own. There are plenty of pieces especially for children. I've performed a number of the ones with narrations, like Prokofiev's *Peter and the Wolf,* Saint-Saëns' *Carnival of the Animals,* and Britten's *The Young Person's Guide to the Orchestra,* and there are plenty of recordings of each. *Peter and the Wolf* is also available in numerous book versions: one recent edition includes pictures of the instruments that portray each character, and the written-out musical theme, as well as lovely illustrations. Non-narration pieces that appeal to children include Leopold Mozart's *Toy Symphony* (pick out the cuckoo clock!).

There are several story audiotapes that focus on classical music. *Beethoven Lives Upstairs, Mr. Bach Comes to Call,* and *Mozart's Magic Fantasy* provide imaginative story frameworks for music by these composers. Produced for six-year-olds to adults, they have been known to captivate even two-and-a-half-year-olds. *The Orchestra* by Mark Rubin is available on videotape, or as a cassette with a book, and features Peter Ustinov introducing the instruments of the orchestra and musical concepts; the video version simply photographs the illustrations, rather than using live performers. The

Rochester Philharmonic has put out a similar tape, with book, called *My First Concert*. These tapes, and others, are available from "Music for Little People."

But you need not limit your children's records to "kids' music." When Kara, Teddy, and Patrick got older, they had their own tape players, and for birthdays and Christmas I gave them classical tapes. I still do. I wouldn't necessarily even wait for a holiday; I'd just say, "Here's a new tape I love" and hand it over. Half the time, they didn't know what they were listening to, but they liked it. Teenagers spend two hours a night in their rooms with the door closed. I know my kids played a lot of rock during those hours, but the tapes gave them a choice. When Patrick was about thirteen, he liked Debussy's *La Mer* (The Sea). Debussy's music sounds like the ocean, and Patrick always said that it helped him to have it playing quietly while he was reading a book, studying, or doing his homework. He was also partial to Vivaldi's *The Four Seasons*. Your kids' tastes may surprise you. Young children especially are lucky to have fewer preconceived ideas about classical music than adults have, and they may respond to the percussive, nontonal, nonlinear excitement of some contemporary music that people brought up on a diet of Beethoven and Brahms find harder to understand.

For the next step on the media ladder, many concerts and operas are now available on videocassette. Your local video store or library should have some available for rental, or you can order them. Some are for children, like Oliver Knussen's *Where the Wild Things Are,* a delightful musical version of the Maurice Sendak classic, with stage designs by the artist. Others, while not specifically for children, may attract them anyway. Your three-year-old probably won't want to watch Puccini's *La Bohème* from beginning to end, but she may find the action and the music interesting in short doses.

Once you've started, keep it up. Bring your tape player to the playground. Play classical music in the car as you go to the supermarket and to school. I used to have it on when I drove the kids' carpool—when my children were older, we would make deals about so many minutes of classical in exchange for so many minutes of rock during the trips. Other mothers told me that their children commented on it, and they thanked me.

The radio, records, tapes, compact discs, and videos can all be very helpful in getting you and your child ready for the next step, which is the live performance. But all the activities at home aren't just preparatory; they're an enjoyable way of living with music every day and making it part of everyday life. As you participate in musical activities with your children—which will soon include going to concerts, and perhaps even musical classes or instrument lessons—you'll find a richness in the sharing of a wonderful experience. Most musicians found their way into their profession through nurturing parents and teachers. Although your aim is not to produce an artist—though you might—fostering the sense of joy in music happens in the same way.

EIGHT

Going to a Concert

WHEN MY YOUNGEST CHILD, Patrick, was fourteen, the two of us lived together in Boston. Ted and I had separated, the two older children were in college, and Patrick was going to Fessenden and later Andover, living at school during the week and staying with me on weekends. What do you do with a fourteen-year-old boy—especially a Kennedy boy—on weekends? Sports. You go to basketball games, hockey games, and baseball games. I had never paid much attention to sports, apart from the obligatory Kennedy touch football, but suddenly I found myself, in my forties, watching the Boston Celtics play basketball, and at the Boston Garden mystified by my first-ever ice hockey game. I didn't know which side was which, where the puck was supposed to end up, or who was a forward and who was a guard. Patrick and his friends were very patient and explained it all to me, starting with "Look,

Mom, the goalie is the guy in the net with all that padding on" and progressing, as I got more experienced, to more complicated rules and maneuvers.

It got so that I really enjoyed those games, especially baseball at Fenway Park. In each case, it wasn't just the sport; it was the whole experience. I'd buy my Coke and peanuts and hot dog and sit out there in the stands watching all the people as much as the game. It was a visual experience, an olfactory experience; it was being outdoors, hearing the noise of the crowd. I've never understood those people who sit up in air-conditioned glass boxes, separated not only from the field or the rink and the players, but from the people around them as well. If I'm going to a live game, I want to sit down there in the front row where the dust comes off the grass. I want to feel and touch and smell everything. Otherwise, I might as well stay home and watch it on television, which is not the same experience at all.

Concerts have that same immediacy. Whether you sit in a theater, in an opera house, in a church, or even on a blanket in the park, the performers are coming out to play for you, right at that moment. The violin bow is hitting the string as you're watching, not in some studio six months ago. If the pianist misses an entrance, or the French horn cracks, that's it—it's part of that particular performance being created for you. You hear it happening, and you watch it happening. I like to see the body language signals that the concertmaster sends to the players sitting behind him or her, the eye contact between the conductor and soloist, or the cues bouncing around from player to player in a string quartet. I like to watch the conductor sweat. And when it's a really great performance, there's nothing like the feeling of having been there, and having shared that experience with the other people around you.

Music is a living thing. It's not just printed notes on the

page; it's different every time. Any performer will tell you that even a work she's played a hundred times—the Beethoven Violin Concerto, for instance—always has new secrets to reveal. And the rapport between players and audience that only exists in live performance fuels that discovery. It's great to have records at home, but to be in direct contact with the people who are making the music adds a whole different dimension, an electricity.

Over the years, I have taken dozens of friends, young and old, to the opera, the symphony, and chamber music concerts for the first time, and I found it to be one of the musical experiences I enjoy most. Suddenly, things I take for granted are questions for someone else. Why are there so many people in the orchestra for one piece, and so few for another? Who decides what music will be played? Can you really hear a soloist all the way at the back of the hall since there's no amplification? What is the conductor really doing up there? When I see a concert through the eyes of someone who has never been there before, I realize how odd it can all appear, and I find that I don't always know the answers to their questions.

A concert is an environment like any other—a basketball game, a political rally, a birthday party. It has its rules, its traditions, its language. The concert hall itself may be an opulent palace built in the 1800s, or a postmodern architectural statement from the year before last; the soloist may be fifteen years old or eighty; the repertoire from the fourteenth century, or something entirely new. Still, certain characteristics remain consistent, and once you've cracked the environment, you know, on the most basic level, what to expect.

I'd like to take you to a concert. Let's make it in New York, at Carnegie Hall, but it could really be anywhere. The questions—and a lot of the answers—are the same.

Symphony Hall, home of the Boston Symphony, is my usual haunt. I subscribe to the orchestra's concerts, which means I pay for and therefore have my tickets for the entire season, September to May, in advance. Since the orchestra publishes its full list of programs when it advertises subscriptions, I also know in advance what music will be played and what conductors and soloists will perform. I buy two subscriptions for a total of twelve concerts, but it is possible to purchase subscriptions with fewer concerts, and one can almost always buy a ticket to a single event, which is what I do when I travel to other cities.

When I am planning to visit New York, I usually check advance schedules to see what is on at Carnegie Hall or the Metropolitan Opera. If there is something I'd like to hear, I can order tickets over the phone with a credit card, or by mail with a check, or I can have a friend buy them at the box office. I decide where I'd like to sit and how much I want to spend—sometimes, I don't have a choice, so I take what's available. Carnegie Hall, like most concert halls, has a wide range of ticket prices. For a regular event, such as a solo recital or an orchestral concert, you can pay $45 or $50 to sit up front, or $12 for a spot in the top balcony; big attractions, like a performance with lots of soloists, may run much higher—up to $85 or $100 for a ticket, though still with less expensive ($15 or $20) possibilities. Concert halls outside New York have similar ranges, though smaller cities may have lower top prices. (The Minnesota Orchestra's single tickets at home, for example, range from $10 to $32.) For this visit, let's say we're going to hear a visiting midwestern orchestra, conducted by its music director, which is playing Carnegie as part of its East Coast tour.

Orchestras determine their schedules and repertoire far ahead of the concert dates. At least a year in advance, the orchestra administration has begun to look at the possibilities. In the early days of orchestras in the United States, the conductor decided what music he wanted to play, and that was it. Today, orchestras play year-round, and the orchestra's music director conducts only about half of the concerts, if that, so others are involved in the selection. The conductor usually has the first word—and the last. He decides what pieces he most wants to do, and which soloists and guest conductors he would like to invite to perform with the orchestra. These guests must be contracted for far in advance, because well-known artists' schedules fill up quickly. (Opera schedules are set even further in advance because singers and conductors must commit weeks or even months to rehearsals for opera productions.) The soloist or guest conductor may be invited for a particular repertoire specialty, and the exact piece is negotiated. He or she may also be expected to fit into the repertoire gaps left by the music director.

When the conductor has expressed his repertoire preferences, there are still many other factors. What is the balance of eighteenth-, nineteenth-, and twentieth-century music in each program, over the entire season, or over the last several seasons and those to come? What composer hasn't been done enough, or too much? Is the orchestra planning to record any repertoire? Does a particularly desirable guest insist on a particular piece that someone else was planning to do? If the orchestra is going to be touring, the pieces that the conductor wants to show off in other cities should be programmed at home as close as possible to the tour dates.

My friend Jean and I arrive at Carnegie Hall half an hour before the concert time of 8 P.M. Carnegie Hall is a beautiful old building, opened in 1891, with an exterior of soft, reddish terra-cotta stone and a vaulting, elegant auditorium of cream and gold. It has become legendary because of its splendid acoustics—meaning the fidelity and richness with which sound is transmitted from the performers to the listeners—

and its proud history. When it was built, its 57th Street location was a distant outpost of carriage barns and farmlands. Today, it is in the heart of the city, with skyscrapers rearing up around it and a subway running underneath. Still, Central Park is only two blocks away, a reminder of its quasi-rural beginnings.

We leave our coats in the checkroom—I find it very distracting to sit with a lot of fabric on my lap for two hours—and head for the auditorium. People are beginning to stream in the doors, where the ticket takers stand, and down the aisles. Standing on the ground floor (at most theaters, it is called the "orchestra" level; at Carnegie, it is called the "parquet"), you can look upward at the tiers that circle the back of the hall, rising to the cream-colored ceiling with its circlet of lights. Many listeners swear that the best sound in the house is to be heard in the balcony at the very top, where the prices are lowest, too. Getting up there used to involve a stiff climb; when the hall was restored and renovated in 1986, elevators were installed.

The vast stage stretches the entire width of the auditorium. There is no curtain. The musicians' chairs and music stands are in full view, arranged in a semicircular formation, with the conductor's podium front and center. As the concert time approaches, the players enter from the wings carrying their instruments—if they are portable!—and take their seats. The men are dressed in the traditional white tie and tails; women have a bit more sartorial freedom, as long as they fit in with the basic black and white. The players tune or practice tricky passages. Early arrivals can get a little preview of the evening's music from one player's point of view.

Arriving early also gives you a chance to see how the orchestra is assembled. (There is an orchestral seating chart in this book's Appendix.) The loudest instruments are grouped at the rear of the stage. In the back left corner as you face the stage is the battery of percussion instruments. It includes timpani, also known as kettledrums, which can be tuned to different pitches. Beside them, depending on the piece that is to be played, you might see a terrific variety of instruments played with mallets, such as the xylophone, vibraphone, or glockenspiel, drums of all sizes and configurations, and any other instrument that is struck, such as wood blocks, cymbals, or the triangle. Composers can use these instruments for rhythmic emphasis, accents, and all manner of coloristic effects. Many contemporary composers have a wonderful time exploring the possibilities of the percussion section. Nearby are the keyboards, such as piano and the silvery-sounding celesta, which are only occasionally heard as orchestral instruments.

Also at the back of the stage are the brass instruments, so called because they are made of brass and other alloys. Trombones change pitch with their long slides, and big tubas make the lowest sounds, while trumpets are the highest in pitch. French horns, with their coiled bodies and mournful sounds, are also brass instruments, though they join woodwind quintets for chamber music. Brass players make their sound by pressing their lips into the mouthpiece of their instruments. Players who sit in front of the brass section sometimes find its volume difficult to bear, so some orchestras place high Plexiglas shields on the backs of the players' chairs to cut the sound a bit.

In front of the brass and percussion sections are the woodwinds, so called because they were once made all of wood. But modern flutes, held sideways and played by blowing air across the mouthpiece, are made of metal, which gives them a more powerful and piercing sound than their historical counterparts. Other woodwinds are still made of wood, though they have metal keys and fittings. Clarinetists make their sound by blowing air through a single wood reed in the mouthpiece. Oboes, English horns, bassoons, and contrabassoons have two reeds. All woodwind players change pitch by manipulating the length of the column of air through the opening or closing the holes in the instrument with their fingers. If all the holes are closed, the column of air is longer, and the note is lower.

Ranged across the front of the stage, in a wide fan shape, are the instruments of the string family. String players make up more than half the orchestra, because there is strength in numbers—they need to be numerous in order to balance the louder, more piercing sounds of the other instrument families. Most orchestra stringed instruments have four metal strings which are plucked by the right hand or sounded with a wooden bow strung with horsehair that is held in the right hand, while the fingers of the left hand change position on the strings, changing the pitch. The violins, at the left of the stage, are the smallest and the highest in pitch. They are divided into two sections, first and second violins, because they play different parts in the music. The violas, at the center, are somewhat larger instruments and lower in pitch, and the sequence continues with the cellos, on the right, which are still larger and lower, and the basses, behind them at the side of the stage, which are largest and lowest of all. Violins and violas are held under the chin. Cellos, perched on a metal pin, stand upright, gripped between the seated player's knees, while basses are so large that the performer plays either standing up or seated on a high stool. Behind the violins are the harps (if required for the performance), which have forty-seven strings that may be plucked or strummed.

The strings are the heart of the orchestra, the instruments that composers have historically found to be the most versatile and expressive. Orchestral composers of the seventeenth century, like Antonio Vivaldi, or the eighteenth, such as George Frideric Handel, Franz Joseph Haydn, or Wolfgang

Amadeus Mozart, concentrated on music for massed strings, using woodwinds only for occasional color. Stringed instruments provide the greatest range. And because they are played with a bow, they also replicate best a quality associated with the human voice: the ability to join one note to another seamlessly, called "legato."

Orchestra concerts usually last about two hours, including a twenty-minute intermission. That means that the average concert has just over an hour and a half of music, which can be divided in various ways. Sometimes the entire concert will be taken up by a single, huge work, such as Berlioz's *The Damnation of Faust.* More usually, the concert opens with a short work, such as an overture. The first piece may be followed by a concerto, in which a violinist, pianist, cellist, or other instrumental soloist performs with the orchestra. After the intermission comes a large work for orchestra alone—a symphony, a tone poem, or perhaps a piece with chorus and vocal soloists, such as Mozart's Requiem.

Getting to a concert early gives you a chance to read the program notes. I find them a useful road map for what is to come. Sometimes the notes provide a bit of biographical information about the composer, letting you know at what stage of his life he was writing the piece, what his musical concerns were, and what other works he wrote during the same period. Program notes can also give guideposts to listen for in the music—a big melody in the clarinet halfway through, for example—which can help you hear the form of the piece. The Boston Symphony has such detailed program notes that I sometimes like to get them a day or two before the concert so that I can digest them even before I get to the hall. Some orchestras now routinely send their program notes to subscribers in advance, which I think is a very useful practice. I don't usually like reading the notes while I'm listening to the music—when I'm listening, I want to con-

centrate fully—but sometimes they can be helpful in re-
minding you of where the guideposts are.

It's a few minutes before eight, and now all of the musicians are in their seats, and the last audience members are
racing up the aisles to find theirs. Once the music begins, no
one is allowed to enter the hall, which is one of the reasons
that a short opening piece became such a standard on programs: when it is over, there is a pause that allows latecomers
to be seated. I hate getting stuck in traffic and missing the
opening, so I always leave myself plenty of time.

At eight o'clock—or a few minutes after, when the rest of
the orchestra is seated—the concertmaster walks onstage.
The concertmaster leads the first violins and plays solo passages if such are required. Each of the other sections also has
a principal player who fulfills similar duties in the section.
The concertmaster, however, is an important figure. He or
she may lead the entire string section while the conductor is
occupied with other parts of the orchestra. He is also often
the intermediary between the rest of the orchestra and the
conductor. When the concertmaster appears, the music is
about to begin. He signals the oboist, who plays a single long
note—the pitch is A—so that the rest of the orchestra can
tune their instruments to it.

Now the conductor walks onstage through the violins
from the wings, carrying his baton. He reaches the podium, a
raised box with a music stand in front of it at the front and
center of the stage (some conductors work from memory,
dispensing with score and stand altogether), and bows to
acknowledge the audience's applause. He then turns to the
orchestra, and as the audience falls silent, he raises his arms
to give the beat that will signal the orchestra to begin. The
members of the orchestra keep their eyes on him rather than
the audience, because he sets the tempo, signals difficult entrances and rhythm changes, and holds the performance to-

Eugene Ormandy, who was the Philadelphia Orchestra's conductor for thirty-five years, lets me hold the baton at a rehearsal in 1980. (Louis Hood)

I received a Master's in Education from Lesley College in 1981. My family joins me to celebrate after the graduation ceremony. From left: Patrick, me, Kara, Teddy Jr., and Ted. (Brian Quigley)

My mother-in-law and another lover of music, Rose Kennedy, joins me for a duet at the piano at my home in Hyannis Port. (Ken Regan/Camera 5)

In 1984 I narrated Gunther Schuller's *Journey into Jazz* with the Buffalo Philharmonic. Here I am backstage with Raymond Harvey, the conductor for that performance. (Author's collection)

At my birthday party in Hyannis Port in 1983, I receive my favorite gift: my son Patrick serenades me at the piano, playing the jazz piece "Satin Doll," which he learned expressly for the occasion. It was a wonderful surprise! (Author's collection)

Teddy Jr., who enjoys dancing to all kinds of music, joins me for a dance at the wedding of my niece, Sydney Lawford, in Hyannis Port in 1983. (Dennis Reggie)

I accept the applause of John Williams and the audience at Symphony Hall in Boston after narrating *A Young Person's Guide to the Orchestra* with the Boston Pops in 1983. The next week, I narrated the same piece with the Pops for their traditional July 4 outdoor concert. (John Landers, Jr./The Boston Herald)

I visited China with a research team in 1984. While at the Beijing Conservatory of Music I listened to a five-year-old boy play the cello. (Author's collection)

The conductor and composer Leonard Bernstein was a lifelong friend. Here he sings to me backstage at Symphony Hall in Boston, prior to a gala concert celebrating his Harvard class's fiftieth anniversary in 1989. (Donald Dietz)

The cellist Yo-Yo Ma is another of my musical friends. We smile for the camera at a benefit performance for Young Audiences of Massachusetts in Boston, 1990. (Author's collection)

Dancing is something my whole family loves, including my wonderful new son-in-law. Here we are at Kara's wedding in September 1990 at Hyannis Port: Senator Kennedy and the bride, Michael Allen and me. (Dennis Regie)

gether. Most of the work has been done in rehearsal, but for ninety minutes, the conductor must coordinate and inspire the players to re-create the work of the rehearsal with the extra creative zest that goes with performance.

Tonight's program opens with John Adams' *Short Ride in a Fast Machine,* first played in 1986. Adams, who lives in California, was one of the first minimalists (a composer who uses a great deal of repetition and small increments of change in his music), but he has since expanded his range of technique and expression and become the creator of elaborate orchestral works and operas, including an opera called *Nixon in China*—which is, indeed, about President Richard Nixon's historic visit to Communist China in 1972.

Short Ride in a Fast Machine lives up to its title. It kicks right off with a fanfare that doesn't quite settle into announcement—it sounds nervy and jittering, as though fish were jumping out of it. The orchestra revs itself up by repeating the same bit of tune over and over, with slight changes of register and emphasis that heighten the excitement. Suddenly, the rhythm changes slightly, and more instrumental voices join the fray. The thrill of this gathering force seizes hold of me. It reminds me of skiing—at least the way I ski—starting off fast and never getting that much faster, but always more intense, with the fresh, vigorous energy that comes from staving off the cold. Still tightly rhythmic, the music slows a bit, as if gathering every last ounce of power, and then bursts into a triumphal finale. In just over four minutes, I am out of breath. The audience has been caught up too, and the applause is enthusiastic. The conductor turns to acknowledge it, and then leaves the stage.

Mozart's Piano Concerto No. 21 is next, so the stagehands must quickly change the setup onstage while the audience remains seated. *Short Ride* is played with a large orchestra, but Mozart wrote his piece, in 1785, for a much smaller ensemble. A big eighteenth-century orchestra was less than half the size of a modern one, with its one hundred-plus musicians. Some of Mozart's symphonies don't even have woodwinds. The symphony orchestra, after all, started off as a plaything of the aristocracy, so it was made to sound appropriate in a room—admittedly a room of a castle, so fairly sizeable—not a three-thousand-seat auditorium. The nineteenth century went in for public concerts and bigger audiences, and the composers became interested in a broader range of coloristic effects. More kinds of instruments were added. The number of stringed instruments was increased to balance the new additions, and the instruments themselves were eventually converted from gut to metal strings, giving them greater projection.

When I listen to Mozart, I try to put myself back into another time. Nothing could be further from the icy, thrill-seeking, modern character of the Adams piece. Mozart had a tremendous range of expression too, but he used different means to speak of excitement and tragedy. Yet just as we can read the novels of Dickens or the plays of Shakespeare and understand the thoughts and emotions that those writers of past centuries sought to convey, so also can we hear the thoughts and emotions of Mozart, speaking to us in a language that is his own, but is also universal.

The piano has been brought out and placed at the front of the orchestra, near the front of the stage, so the conductor will have to look back over his left shoulder to communicate with the pianist. The piano soloist has a challenge that other soloists don't: he or she can't put the fiddle under an arm and get on a plane, but must make the best of whatever instrument is in the concert hall. In major cities, soloists have a bit more latitude: most are affiliated with one of the major piano companies, who will allow them to try out instruments in their local showrooms and then ship the one they like to the hall for the concert.

I always sit up a bit more when the soloist comes out. I've been there, and I know those preperformance jitters. In order to come out fresh, I've always needed to get nervous first. It always has to feel like the first time, as though you're interpreting music in a way you never have before. If you think it's routine, the audience will feel that way too. Yo-Yo Ma says that music-making is really storytelling of a very private kind; the performer cannot exist without the audience. Yo-Yo says, "I never play a concert unless I feel I'm in that state where I can share. I'm not going out there to prove to people how well I can play."

Now the conductor returns, and the concerto begins. Mozart's piece is divided into three sections, or movements: the opening "allegro maestoso" (fast, majestic), "andante" (slower, a "walking" pace), and "allegro vivace assai" (fast, quite lively). This is traditional terminology (the words are in Italian), a signal from the composer that gives a basic idea of tempo and character. The fast-slow-fast movement format is typical of concertos from the Baroque period through the present. The most elaborate material occurs in the first movement, which lasts about fourteen minutes, but I can't help waiting for the lovely andante—because I've played it, but also just for itself. The first movement ends; there is a brief pause, without applause, because the sections of the piece are connected and should not be interrupted. Then the andante begins.

It is slow—but not too slow—and the orchestra plays, very simply, the exquisite melody that is the movement's primary, indeed only, material. The melody itself is long, yet it is perfectly proportioned and jewel-like, with a sweet innocence. The orchestra finishes its statement, and then the piano repeats the melody, as if it were so beautiful that it simply had to be said again. This movement was the theme for the movie *Elvira Madigan,* which was all about the unconsummated, yearning love of two young, very innocent people. The music has no guile about it. Nothing is hidden; there are no extremes of dynamics. It is idealized romance rather than grand passion, yet as the melody is repeated over and over again, barely changed, it never becomes tiresome. There are no flashy finger moves in the piano part (one of the reasons that an amateur like me would dare play it in a concert), yet you can't get away with thinking it's easy. You have to breathe it just right, so that its tenderness speaks.

The orchestra and the piano take turns: sometimes the soloist is featured, sometimes the orchestra. This is a pure example of the "classical" balance that exists in this kind of eighteenth-century music. Melody is what counts here, and questions and answers. The piano and the orchestra are not challenging each other, as they often do in concertos written by later composers, such as Tchaikovsky or Rachmaninoff. They are in peaceful, unfolding coexistence. In the Adams piece, everything was working toward a visceral, rhythmic excitement. In the Mozart, all the piano and the orchestra want to do is sing.

When the movement is over, the magic endures for a moment. There is no coughing, no rustling, just a chance to sigh and live in the wonderful, contemplative world that Mozart created for just a little bit longer. Then the orchestra begins the final movement, reintroducing a speedier, jaunty character. It still sounds nothing like the Adams piece, however: two hundred years make a considerable difference.

The concerto, which has lasted about half an hour, concludes the first half of the program. It is followed by an intermission, which gives the musicians a rest and the audience members a chance to stretch their legs and talk to their friends. Concerts are a wonderful social opportunity. You are always aware of the fact that you are listening to music with others. The lights in the house are not turned off, as they are in the theater or at the opera. The stage is more brilliantly lit than the audience, but you can still see who is around you, or follow the texts in the program, if it is a choral or vocal concert.

Of course, concerts are social in the usual sense too: you can also talk to your friends during the intermissions or listen to what other people have to say about the concert. If I go to a concert alone, sometimes I talk to the people sitting next to me—especially in Symphony Hall, where the couple in the adjoining seats has been going to the Boston concerts for far longer than I have. I like going to concerts with friends because we can share a stimulating experience and talk about it halfway through, just as you can when going to the theater. My son Teddy used to find concerts a wonderful way of dating. The girls were very impressed, and it gave them common ground for conversation, especially if they didn't know each other well. Teddy says, "It was more special than just going to another teenage rock concert, because it wasn't something that everybody did, and there was a kind of mystique about it. So I would appear very cultured, we could both get dressed up, and the sound of all those musicians banging away at their instruments all at the same time was really exhilarating!"

The intermission also gives you the opportunity to read the rest of the program notes. This concert's second half will be entirely devoted to the Symphony No. 4 in E minor of Brahms. Composers have fashions with conductors and audiences, but Brahms, like Beethoven, is evergreen. Some composers are only recently popular. Shostakovich is in vogue now. You'll find many young conductors recording him and putting his symphonies on their programs. Mahler is another favorite, due very much to the influence of Leonard Bernstein. When Mahler died in 1911, his music was seldom played. The symphonies are emotional and sometimes extremely long. But Bernstein loved Mahler and started to play him at the New York Philharmonic, when he was music director there from 1958 to 1969, and in his guest conducting visits with other orchestras, and conductors started to catch on. Now, every young conductor feels as though he has to prove himself with Mahler.

Now the conductor returns to the podium to begin. He isn't using a score—an amazing feat, considering that he has to have all the parts in his head. For some conductors, it's a stunt; for others, the score is as distracting as a script would be for an actor in performance.

Brahms wrote this symphony, his last, between 1884 and 1885. It has four movements and lasts about forty minutes. We are in a different world of sound and sense than we were with Adams or Mozart, and in Brahms we hear a master orchestrator manipulate themes and choirs of instruments for all sorts of theatrical and emotional effects. Yet Brahms still hewed to the Classical layout of the symphony, with the important opening statement in the first movement, the slower second movement, the dancelike scherzo third, and a finale to bring it all to a close.

The opening of the first movement is simple and forthright, a broad, relaxed melody played expansively by the strings. Then there is a change of mood—a horn calls out, offering yet another theme, and then comes still another. This is a big orchestra, yet nothing is loud—we just have a sense of mass and possibility which still creates a very gentle, pastoral mood. Themes are played, are modified, disappear, and return. The whole orchestra plays, and then suddenly the texture thins out, so that only the clarinets can be heard. The central focus, or tonality, shifts from minor to major and then back again, setting up an emotional ambiguity. Is it happy and assertive, or questioning? As he changes, Brahms is propelling us along, setting up our ears to expect the return of that first theme. A little more than halfway through, we hear it again, resolving the ambiguity, and sense that we are on the home stretch.

But Brahms doesn't leave it there. He always gives something new. The cello section plays a theme. Then come the horns and trumpets, loud and penetrating, with a brassy timbre that contrasts with the vibrating cellos. Suddenly, the string players pluck their instruments in unison instead of bowing. This symphony is all about contrast—loud with soft, major with minor, pastoral with martial, stringy colors with brassy or woodwind ones. Yet order prevails, because it is also about repetition and the psychological expectation that something will be heard again. One minute from the end, the first theme bursts out again (repetition), but this time it is very agitated (contrast), propelling you toward the ending. And then Brahms surprises us once again by ending it all with a slow drum roll. I'm still on the edge of my seat, waiting for that ending, because instead of rounding out the movement as Mozart would have done, Brahms has set us up for the next movement.

In the rest of the piece, Brahms keeps up the pace, setting up expectations and delaying or transforming their resolutions so that you stay with him. The second movement vibrantly recalls the first because the horns that made only a token appearance before are now front and center. This time, the music is slow and unambiguously pastoral, focusing on woodwind choirs rather than strings. Then comes the third movement, the shortest, Brahms' only symphonic scherzo, which erupts in ebullient, extroverted high spirits and exploits the contrast between the growling full orchestra and a tingling triangle. The majestic finale, which features a lovely flute solo at the center, returns us to the unsettled mood of the opening. Like that first movement, it ends with a question rather than a statement. Grand and passionate as it is, the symphony is monumental without being smug. I feel a very human, struggling intelligence in Brahms.

By the end, I am exhausted. There is nothing quite like the sound of a great orchestra. It commands a purely visceral excitement of the kind you can get listening to a rock band or driving a fast car, if that is what you like. Great orchestras are always being compared to Rolls-Royces—magnificent, well-oiled machines with thousands of moving parts, all of which work together to perfection. The sound can be like a great cushion or an electrical storm vibrating in the air around you. It brings you along with it, showing you the route of the composer's thoughts and making you feel his emotions at the same time. I can understand why conductors like their jobs. It's hard work. There are purely musical and intellectual choices faced at every turn: How fast should this passage be? What beat should have the accent? Are the strings and the woodwinds balanced in their sound? The conductor also has to translate his decisions to the orchestra just using his face and his body. Yet the conductor has a huge, highly trained, beautifully flexible machine as his instrument. He controls it, summons the whispering pianissimos and thundering climaxes, balances the choirs, is the intermediary between the composer and the audience. It's no wonder that conductors tend to live a long time.

The concert is over. We've applauded, brought the conductor back to the stage, and seen the orchestra bow and bow again, and now we're filing back down the aisles in search of coats, cars, and home. I'm always fired up after a concert. Musical passages swim up into my mind; the emotions they produced—daredevil in Adams, gentle in Mozart, cataclysmic and overpowering in Brahms—return and haunt me, and I give myself up to them with joy.

. . . .

Children can feel the electricity of live concerts as much as adults do. They are caught up first in the excitement of going out, of dressing up and having a special occasion, but if what's happening on the stage is good, it grabs them too. I used to take my children, their cousins, and their friends to concerts and the ballet. At first it was as strange for them as going to sports events was for me, but they adapted quickly.

For us, there were all sorts of possibilities: Tchaikovsky's *Nutcracker* ballet at Christmastime, musicals in the Melody Tent during our summers in Hyannis Port, birthday outings, or just a concert that I thought one or more of the kids might enjoy.

For instance, right around the time of my first hockey game in Boston, I took Patrick to hear the great tenor Luciano Pavarotti sing a recital. Patrick wasn't sure about the idea. He thought we were going to the opera, and he'd heard that operas were long and boring, but to please me, he agreed to go.

The Wang Center in Boston was packed with people of all ages, including his. Pavarotti sang a program of the most famous tenor arias, some of the most thrilling music there is. Pavarotti is an extraordinary performer, and his voice is an amazing instrument; Patrick couldn't believe how high and powerful it was, and yet at the same time so caressing and lyrical. Pavarotti is a huge man, and when he performs he sweats profusely, clutches the big white handkerchief that has become his signature prop, and flings his arms wide at the end of every number, as though he were going to embrace the whole hall. One might expect a teenager to find the whole thing absurd, but Patrick didn't in the least. The recital built in intensity, and by the final encore—the glorious aria "Nessun dorma" from Puccini's *Turandot,* in which Calaf swears that his love will conquer the icy, murderous, but beautiful Princess Turandot—Patrick was totally enchanted. He insisted on going backstage to meet Pavarotti afterward. I knew he'd really gotten the bug when he told Kara and Teddy Jr. about it and got them all excited about hearing Pavarotti too. So of course I took them, and they reported on the experience to their father, which even inspired him to buy some Pavarotti tapes.

The trick with any beginner is to pick the right event. Patrick loved Pavarotti, but I don't think I would have taken him to that concert when he was six. Instead, I probably would have chosen an orchestral concert or chamber music concert designed especially for children, or an outdoor event where he could run around. The same goes for adults choosing a first concert for themselves. There are so many possibilities that with a little judicious research, it should be a simple matter to come up with the right match.

Concerts exist everywhere. There's no need to go to a major city like New York, Boston, or Chicago. The first step is to find out who your local ensembles and presenters are. A "presenter" may be an orchestra, an opera company, or an institution like a concert hall (Carnegie Hall, for example), theater, church, or chamber music series which decides what performers to bring to town, or which local performers to present. The presenter pays the musicians, publicizes the concert, sells the tickets, and runs the event. Some presenters overlap: an orchestra, in addition to its own series of concerts, may sponsor a series of visiting soloists or chamber groups. Colleges and universities are an excellent source for concerts. Many bring soloists and ensembles to town, as well as presenting their own students and faculty members. Student concerts also have the advantage of being free. Museums often present chamber music series: the Isabella Stuart Gardner Museum in Boston has one that I am especially fond of, because I enjoy the juxtaposition of music and paintings. Many concerts are not presented by big operators; these are best found by the flier/word-of-mouth/bulletin board method. There may be a tiny new music group that presents its own concerts in a church, or a period instruments ensemble that focuses exclusively on the music of the seventeenth century. Don't limit your options: you never know what might turn you on.

Churches offer another terrific possibility for listening. I tend to shop around for Sunday services, checking the music offerings of churches in the Boston area. There is a tremendously rich body of church music, and it's thrilling to hear it in the context for which it was originally written, rather than in a concert hall. One of my favorite musical venues is Boston's Emmanuel Church, which has a terrific group of singers led by its music director, Craig Smith. It isn't a Catholic church, so I don't make it my regular Sunday observance, but I try to go several times a year to hear their Bach cantatas and other musical offerings. I'm also partial to St. Paul's Catholic Church in Cambridge, where I get goose bumps listening to the Archdiocesan Boys' Choir sing the 11 A.M. mass.

Concerts were once limited to the winter months, but now that most halls are air-conditioned, and orchestras need to play year-round to provide enough work for their musicians, summer festivals have exploded all around the country, and it is possible to find live music at virtually any time of the year.

What kind of concert do you start with? If you are concerned about the formality of regular concerts—dress, protocol, expense, and so on—one of the best first experiences is the more relaxed environment of an outdoor (often free) concert.

Most cities offer some kind of outdoor musical event during the summer, whether it's a band concert, a wind serenade, or a whole orchestra floating on a barge, like the pops concert that the John F. Kennedy Library presented one summer in Boston Harbor. The lure of music alfresco has grown in recent years. There are now dozens of festivals, and many orchestras have summer seasons in outdoor facilities. One of the oldest is the famous Tanglewood Festival in the Berkshires of western Massachusetts, where for twelve dollars every weekend all summer long, you can sit on the grass under the stars and hear the Boston Symphony, to say nothing of the crack student orchestra and ensembles of the Tanglewood Music Center. I also love to go to the summer pops concerts on the Boston Esplanade; and when Kara was living in Boston, before she married and moved to Washington, she was also an Esplanade fan. She and her then-fiancé Michael would get some friends together, take a picnic, and get down to the river as the sun was setting. She says, "The place would be full of all kinds of people, young and old, families with small children. You could still see people jogging or bicycling by, or sailing up the Charles. We'd sit halfway down the green from the orchestra, and just relax and listen to the music as the sun went down."

At outdoor concerts, you can often bring a picnic lunch or supper, spread out a few blankets, invite your friends, wear whatever you like, and make listening to music an informal party. You can bring your kids, and they don't have to sit still in chairs. Babies can sleep in a carriage or stroller, and if they cry, it's not a tragedy. A friend of mine brought her ten-month-old daughter to Tanglewood one summer; the baby spent the whole time crawling over to other people's blankets and clinging to their picnic coolers, and nobody seemed to mind.

Older children can listen to the music or play if their attention wanders—and if it wanders too far for everyone's comfort, you can leave without causing any fuss or embarrassment. This sort of concert is also a terrific opportunity to teach your kids something about music: you can take them up to the stage and show them the instruments and musicians, and point out the sounds of particular instruments while the music is playing. Outdoor concerts also have a community spirit about them. They are full of people who might never go to a concert hall. Programs tend to feature fairly accessible music, which goes with the relaxed atmosphere.

The Esplanade concerts are usually pops programming; Tanglewood and other orchestra summer homes like Ravinia (the Chicago Symphony) or Blossom (the Cleveland Orchestra) have more variety. The Boston Symphony features standard works with famous soloists (Itzhak Perlman playing Beethoven's magnificent Violin Concerto, for example), but less familiar fare gets programmed as well. One summer, Tanglewood presented Benjamin Britten's powerful *War Requiem,* one of the most poignant antiwar statements ever made in music. Thus, Tanglewood is a useful way to get a wide-ranging musical introduction.

Other outdoor concerts are free: the New York Philharmonic and the Metropolitan Opera perform in the parks of all five New York City boroughs every summer. People stake out spots on Central Park's Great Lawn early in the morning, and they stay the whole day, hearing the rehearsals and the sound checks. Not all outdoor concerts are standard repertoire either: New York's Museum of Modern Art has programmed twentieth-century chamber music concerts in its sculpture garden. Imagine listening to Arnold Schoenberg's weird, pointillistic *Pierrot Lunaire* in counterpoint with every bird in New York. In Minneapolis, the Minnesota Orchestra's annual Viennese Sommerfest takes place inside its downtown concert hall, but outside there is an Austrian "marketplace" with food booths and hours of music played by everything from wind quintets to oompah bands.

To find out about such events, call the office of your local orchestra, your chamber of commerce, or the classical radio station. Check newspapers and bulletin boards, and ask around. If you live near an orchestra's summer home, call and find out about programs, and ask how much lawn tickets cost.

Another good first option, for children and adults, is a short concert. Many orchestras in particular offer family concerts, geared for parents and children, on weekend mornings or afternoons. Most are about an hour long, right for young attention spans. The orchestras may perform children's classics, like *Peter and the Wolf,* or newer works written especially for children. Another kind of program features short selections, or movements of concertos or symphonies, from the classical repertoire.

Some family concerts use some kind of visual device as well, like an actor, a musician, a mime, slides, drawing, and all kinds of props. The conductor ties the program together in some way—through commentary, demonstration, games—and can often illuminate the music in a way that will appeal even to the seasoned concertgoer.

I love family concerts. They're extremely entertaining, and the Boston Symphony's, at least, never fail. I've gone with friends (male and female) and their children or grandchildren, and they always enjoy them. I remember one that was a big hit—it featured ballet music and had dancers, who added a visual component and demonstrated their special art on a tiny portion of the stage. I've also taken friends without children who didn't feel ready for a full-scale evening concert to the Boston Symphony's family concerts, and they were perfect: just long enough, unintimidating, and terrific music. Orchestras offer children's concerts during the week for schools as well—you might want to try some of those, perhaps by volunteering to usher.

Museums are also starting to recognize the possibilities inherent in short concerts. The Isabella Stuart Gardner Museum's chamber music programs are short—just an hour or so, without intermission—and the Metropolitan Museum in New York has started a similar series on Friday nights. This works for the museums, who want patrons to go around and look at the art as well as listen to the music, and for listeners who would rather have a shorter, more intense musical experience.

When you're ready for the full-length concert, shop around. You may want a program that offers more than music: orchestras are now recognizing that some concertgoers—or potential concertgoers—would like a little more guidance through the repertoire, so they are offering special concerts, geared toward adults, that include some discussion of the works performed. Sometimes regular concerts, especially those with contemporary music on them, have pre-concert lectures included in the ticket price: you just come an hour or half an hour early.

Another aid for the uninitiated has recently been instituted in opera houses: supertitles. If you've watched non-English language movies with subtitles, you know how it works. In the opera house, translations of the text are projected on a screen above the stage, and a quick glance upward gives the gist of what's going on. Even regular opera goers like supertitles: even those who know the librettos well or have read them beforehand find it difficult to remember every nuance of text and story. Operas were written for people who understood the language in which they were being performed. Many people feel that translation of the sung text violates the integrity of its relationship with the music, so supertitles represent a fine compromise.

Pops concerts can offer a possible introduction to classical music. Pops is really a genre of its own, geared toward entertainment, with lights, costumes, conductors who address the audience, and sometimes nightclub-style performers who use the orchestra as a sonic backup. But the pops concert as pioneered by Arthur Fiedler at the Boston Pops was intended to be an evening featuring "light" classics—overtures or colorful, popular works like Sibelius's *Finlandia* or Ravel's *Boléro*—concertos with young performers, and symphonic arrangements of popular tunes. Fiedler hoped that pops goers would eventually become symphony goers. Many orchestras still do some concerts in the format he pioneered. Most do some sort of pops, and if your local orchestra is geared toward light classical repertoire rather than big stars, you can at least get an introduction to the language of the music that you would hear in a regular symphony concert.

In choosing a regular concert, remember your at-home listening, as set out in Chapter Seven: Who were the composers who interested you? Did you like orchestral music particularly? Did you like string quartets? Singers? Works with solo piano? Look at the concert schedules of your town's presenters, call a local college or university to see what's on (faculty and student performances are not usually determined as far in advance as other kinds of concerts), and pick a performance that has some frame of reference for you. Most orchestral programs include an overture or a short opening piece, a concerto, and then, after intermission, a symphony or other large work. A solo instrumental recital or chamber music program may have five or six pieces on it, a song recital many more, so there is bound to be a piece or at least a composer that you recognize. If you're feeling really adventurous, pick an all-new-music program, or a concert with works you've never heard of—you never know what may prove to be stimulating.

If you find out in advance what the program is—which you can almost always do, and it's worth the trouble—you can borrow recordings from the library or buy them at a record store and become familiar with them. I've often found that audiences are extra attentive to pieces they know well: the delighted reaction when I played the slow movement from Mozart's Piano Concerto No. 21 (the one used in *Elvira Madigan*) is a case in point. Alternatively, you may decide that you would rather be surprised and not prepare at all. If you're going to an opera which is to be sung in a foreign language, however, it's a very good idea to read the libretto, or at least a synopsis of the story, first.

You may be able to get tickets by mail, charge them over the phone on a credit card, or just walk up to the box office and buy them a few weeks or days before the concert. Most concerts have a range of prices. Call or check newspaper ads to find out about availability, and don't assume you can get tickets on the day of the concert. As with any performing medium, tickets to performances by very famous artists sell out quickly.

Dress is up to you. For an evening concert, you probably will feel out of place if you go in jeans and a T-shirt, but unless it's an opening night gala, there's no need for a fancy dress or a tuxedo, unless you feel like wearing one. Orchestra and chamber musicians usually wear white tie (men) and black skirts or trousers (women), conductors wear tuxedos or tails, and women soloists dress for a cross between effect and comfort (no five-inch heels for the violin soloist, no matter how short she is). This is the European tradition, but the formality only spills over to the audience on special occasions. Even musicians do not always dress formally: some contemporary music groups, like the extremely popular Kronos

Quartet, make their new-wave garb part of their musical statement.

Be sure to leave enough time to get to the hall and park. Latecomers are usually admitted only after the first work or movement to avoid disturbing other audience members, and if you're late for the opera, you'll miss the whole first scene.

Many people worry about when to applaud. In America, it is now customary to applaud only after the complete piece has been played, even though a quartet, concerto, or symphony may be subdivided into several movements, with pauses in between. Of course, rules are made to be broken, and an especially exciting performance will often excite applause—as it should. At the opera, big arias usually call for applause as well. There are various schools of thought about applause that "interrupts" in this way: some audience members (and performers) find that it breaks the mood, but some performers appreciate the recognition. Feel it out for yourself. A gratuitous "bravo" before a beautiful pianissimo (a very soft passage) has ended, for example, is obnoxious, while applause after a really bravura movement is not out of line. At the opera, however, be sure that the last note has died away, rather than beginning to applaud as the curtain begins descending—you may miss something wonderful, and so will the people around you. Talking, coughing, unwrapping candy, and fidgeting are also extremely disturbing to both the performers and the other audience members, and taking photographs or recording is almost always prohibited by law.

Taking children to a full-length concert involves some planning and flexibility. I used to take groups of kids to concerts and the ballet as a birthday party: we'd have as many as fifteen kids and another mother to help. I would also take just one child and a friend—when children have buddies to do something with, it becomes much more fun. Alternatively, if the child is especially fond of a grandparent, or an aunt, a performance might be a special outing that they can do together.

I found that one trick about taking kids to performances was to make sure they had lunch *first*. Another was to sit in the balcony, where they could see everything that was going on onstage and all the rows of orchestral instruments, rather than on the orchestra level, where you can only see the front rows. This is especially useful when little boys are part of the group: Teddy Jr. always liked watching the percussionists, who stand at the back. The visual excitement of an orchestra is a big factor in keeping children interested in the music, so the more they can see, the more possibilities there are.

Another useful strategy is to be prepared to leave at any time. I remember taking a group of little girls to the ballet. By the end of the first hour, each one had had to go to the bathroom, and when that snowball effect happens, all you can do is pick up and go. Kids don't have very long attention spans, so if an hour is all they can take, it's better to have them enjoy that hour and then leave, rather than forcing them through the rest of the performance and making everyone unhappy. Ballet, incidentally, especially a story ballet, is a good introduction to live music for children, because they can focus on the visual.

Try all sorts of concerts and dance. Keep an open mind, just as you did with your record listening. Take a spouse or a friend and make an evening of it; or buy a cheap seat (they often have the best sound, anyway—remember the top balcony of Carnegie Hall), slip in for one or two pieces, and then leave if you've had enough. I'm sure you'll find that a live performance is the ultimate musical experience. Here's testimony from a friend whom I took to the opera for the first time a few years ago.

"My credentials as a non-opera buff were substantial. I grew up in Wichita, Kansas. I was not exposed to the Metropolitan Opera on the radio on Saturday afternoons. My musical career peaked when, at age fourteen, I played the clarinet at a pizza parlor for all the Coke and pizza I could eat. Although I'm told that I went to the opera at Milan's La Scala when I was ten, I remember nothing about it; as a flower child of the sixties, my musical preferences leaned more toward Pink Floyd, the Beatles, early Bob Dylan, and Marvin Gaye.

"I have now seen *Die Fledermaus, Rigoletto, Madama Butterfly, La Bohème,* and *The Marriage of Figaro* with Joan. I prepared by reading the librettos in English and watching videotapes of the operas. To my surprise, the audience was not particularly old or stuffy, nor were the themes outdated —deceit, hypocrisy, love, arrogance, conflicts between races, sexes, and classes are all still with us. There was more character development and certainly more imaginative plotting than in almost any television show or movie I have seen recently. The talent and enthusiasm of the singers was overwhelming. I saw people in the audience, eyes closed, tears running down their cheeks, removed far beyond their daily problems. I was there too.

"So far, my favorite opera has been *Rigoletto.* Backstage at the Metropolitan Opera afterwards, Joan and I were wandering the corridors looking for the exit. Spotting a poster for *The Barber of Seville,* I remembered a line from that opera and burst out with 'Figaro, Figaro, Figaro!' Suddenly, my song was answered by a much better voice. Having responded to my performance, Luciano Pavarotti walked through the door and waited for me to continue. Unfortunately, I had no idea what the next line was, and as I have yet to find a better singing partner, I think I will have to take early retirement from the operatic stage.

"Opera is an acquired taste. The more I learn, the more I

appreciate it. Now, when an opera comes on the radio, I don't automatically change the station to search for Crosby, Stills, and Nash. Instead, I listen for a recognizable aria, a known singer, or familiar scene. I guess I can say it's a taste I've acquired."

NINE

Making Music:
Lessons and Beyond

L IKE MANY PARENTS, I started thinking about music lessons for my children when they were small. Playing and listening were central to my life, and I wanted to be sure they had the opportunity to have that pleasure as well. Certainly there was music in the air in our house, but I wanted Teddy, Kara, and Patrick to have some way to participate as well. So they all took piano lessons, starting when they were about eight. None were especially gifted, as it turned out, and only Patrick continued his studies beyond three or four years, but all three took something away from the experience.

But before you plunge ahead with instrumental lessons and all the attendant questions—which instrument, how old the child should be, how to choose a teacher—I think that it is helpful to think about *why* you want your child to take music lessons, and what you expect from those lessons. My feeling is that music is both a means for expression and community participation and a continual, splendid source of personal enjoyment and enrichment. Composers put emotions and ideas into music because that is the best way they have to communicate them to us. I can only imperfectly say in words what a Mozart symphony, or a Bartók string quartet, or a song by Jerome Kern says to me. If words were really possible, the music wouldn't be necessary.

There are all sorts of routes to that kind of fulfillment through music. Listening is one, and I've talked about how recordings and concerts make that possible. Playing and singing alone, whether for others or simply for oneself, and mastering the techniques required to do so is another. Playing or singing with ensembles, be it with one or two other people, in an orchestra, or in a choir, is another. Composition —from the simplest, untrained improvisations through fully developed creations—is an exciting possibility as well. For many, learning about where music came from, the context in which it was written, and the people who first heard and played it is extremely rewarding. My ideal complete musician, amateur or professional, has had at least a brush with all of these things. If one turns out to be purely a listener, as so many do, the listening will be that much richer for the other experiences.

Instrumental instruction is wonderful and desirable, but it is not the only way to go, and indeed, a narrow preoccupation with it may keep a potential music lover from exploring other possibilities. Waiting for the child to turn eight, dragging him to the neighborhood piano teacher, and waiting eagerly for him to learn a few party pieces—this is a familiar scenario, but not necessarily one that produces rich and happy music-making. Start lessons by all means, but also consider earlier musical experiences—of the sort that tap the child's natural curiosity, playfulness, and love of movement, for example—which may ultimately make for a happier pi-ano or violin student.

Children can do things with music at any age. In Chapter Seven, I wrote about some of the activities that parents and children can do together at home from birth on. If your child has been singing and humming, playing with musical toys or even real musical instruments, inventing his own instru-ments, listening and dancing to recordings and videotapes of all kinds of music (whether it's "Shake Your Sillies Out," Beatles songs, Brahms symphonies, or Olivier Messiaen's musical impressions of birdsong), and, most important, had parents participating in these activities, he will have a head start. Music will be a part of his life—something he *does*—and educational theorists assert that children learn, and un-derstand, by doing.

If you would like to encourage musical experimentation in a more organized setting with your young child, there are many programs that may suit you. Most nursery school pro-grams involve singing and other musical play, so if you look for one that is especially interested in music—geared to ex-ploration rather than lessons or performances—your three- or four-year-old can enjoy musical play in a group setting where she would be anyway.

For more specialized classes, investigate the local college or university. Their music education departments sometimes offer classes, for the benefit of their students' research and practice teaching, that focus on early childhood music educa-tion. Another excellent resource for early childhood music instruction—indeed, for music at all levels—is the commu-nity music schools that exist all over the country. The first of these were founded a century ago to give impoverished im-migrants access to low-cost music education, instrumental instruction, and vocal or instrumental ensemble perfor-mance. New ones have sprung up since, and they flourish today, providing these services and more. The National Guild of Community Schools of the Arts in Englewood, New Jersey, can provide parents with the name of a local school.

Classes vary widely and are geared toward the age of the child. The lower limit is usually two-year-olds, but even younger children are sometimes the focus of such programs. Parents attend the classes with the youngest children; indeed, the classroom teachers may focus on helping parents understand, encourage, and enlarge upon their children's instinctive musical play, on the premise that the parent is the best teacher. Sometimes materials, such as song sheets or toys, are provided for use at home.

Classes for preschoolers are built around play. A group for children under two would probably involve some organized singing and movement activity, as well as free time for the child to investigate a room full of musical toys and games on her own. A group of two- and three-year-olds can manage more sustained group play, which could include singing with finger games, playing with basic instruments such as drums and sticks, and movement to music. A slightly older group could learn basic concepts through games—pitching the voice high or low, for example, or running and walking to learn about tempo. Each class might focus on a particular kind of instrument or musical principle. Older children might make up their own songs or notations.

Music schools that are connected with the local university can enrich their offerings considerably. The McPhail Center for the Arts in Minneapolis, for example, has five different programs for preschoolers, infants to age six, that involve everything from basic music and movement to a course that introduces three-and-a-half- to four-and-a-half-year-olds and their parents to basic musical concepts and skills, to a thirty-three-week course that enables four- and five-year-olds to try out just about every folk and classical musical instrument.

Some programs incorporate listening time; they use either recordings or a pianist or other instrumentalist to supply music. They may feature a wide variety of music—Western classical pieces of many eras, folk music of all kinds, simple children's songs—in a way that gives children a sense of the richness of musical creation and experience, and music's connection to human lives. An Indonesian gamelan orchestra, a Jamaican steel drum, a jazz band, and a string quartet all make wonderful, exotic sounds and speak in different languages. For the child who is creating her own wonderful and exotic sounds, here is a great panoply of aural experience for her to explore.

Many early childhood programs are based on the principles of three music education systems: Dalcroze, Orff, and Kodály, named after their founders. Each seeks to develop a child's (or adult's) innate musicality through rhythm, improvisation, and singing. These theorists felt that the fledgling musician would find it easier to understand the basic principles of music if he or she were not struggling to master the complexities of an instrument at the same time.

Émile Jaques Dalcroze, a Swiss composer and educator who lived from 1865 to 1950, pioneered the system of eurythmics, or the exploration of all musical elements—rhythm, phrasing, form, and more—through physical movement. For Dalcroze, the idea was to *feel* rhythm, for example, rather than simply recognize it. The German composer Carl Orff (1895–1982) developed a family of specialized, easy-to-play instruments, mostly percussion and xylophone-type bar instruments, that enable children to improvise in groups. Zoltán Kodály, the Hungarian composer, ethnomusicologist, and educator (1882–1967), believed that children learned best when lessons grew out of their own culture and their innate abilities. For him, singing—using the child's own instrument, the voice—came first; folk music, which is, of course, related to the child's own language, was the best introduction to music. Kodály's system also incorporates some Dalcroze- and Orff-generated principles, such as movement and using clapping as accompaniment.

Many of these principles are used by music teachers for school-age children and become progressively more sophisticated. But even four- and five-year-olds can sing songs with strong, identifiable rhythms, imitate patterns, recognize and physically act out basic musical notations, play games built around musical themes, and experiment with instruments. Through play built on these basic techniques, children become familiar with musical matters early, grasping whatever they can at their developmental level.

With this sort of grounding, formal study of a musical instrument becomes a new avenue for fun and exploration, rather than an imposed drudgery. Children also acquire the rudiments of improvisation and ensemble participation, skills that make future music education infinitely more rewarding.

So what about that first instrument? When do you start? Some teachers sit children as young as eighteen months at the piano for directed musical play. A teacher might play notes at the piano and sing them to words that are part of the child's world ("Mom-my," "Dad-dy"), then go on to more complex expressions ("Who's your friend?" "Tom-my!").

The age at which a child can go beyond play and actually master an instrument is open to debate. Shin'ichi Suzuki, the Japanese educator, pioneered a system of teaching that has been widely replicated and adapted in the United States. Suzuki believed that very young children could learn instruments in the same way they learn language. He felt that such children were physically better suited than older ones to master instruments, and that indeed, after a certain point, such ability lessened dramatically. Suzuki started three- and four-year-olds on the violin. He showed them the hand positions and tapped their considerable imitative skills. Suzuki-trained youngsters listened to a teacher or a tape and exactly replicated the pitches they were hearing, thus developing ear training. They progressed, through a set curriculum, from "Twinkle, Twinkle, Little Star" through an entire concerto. Most of the music was learned through imitation (Suzuki introduced the concept of note reading later) and in groups. Suzuki programs often field large groups of astonishingly small children playing note-perfect versions of very advanced repertoire.

The other integral aspect of Suzuki's teaching was the participation of the parent. Suzuki believed that children want to do what their parents do, that if they see a parent learning the violin or the cello, they will clamor for lessons as well. In the ideal Suzuki model, child and parent go to lessons together, and at home, they play for each other and are intimately involved in each other's practice. The study of the instrument becomes a sharing, pleasurable experience for parent and child.

In America, the Suzuki method has been slightly modified. For example, note reading often starts earlier, private lessons are available, and parents, given the stresses on adults here, are not always required to take lessons—though they usually participate in them, and the practice sessions, with very young children. (The child may also be starting instrumental lessons at a time when the last thing in the world they want is parent participation—and competition—so it is important to be sensitive to that in choosing a teacher or method.) Other early childhood techniques are incorporated into Suzuki teaching too, so that while the emphasis remains early technical mastery, basic musical skills are taught through the kinds of games mentioned earlier. Teachers who use the method may be found in Suzuki schools (such as the School for Strings in New York), in departments of larger music schools, or in their own private studios.

One advantage of the Suzuki technique is that the child physically masters the technicalities of the instrument very early. The Suzuki method is also very gratifying to parents, because the child very quickly has something to show for all the money and hours spent on music lessons.

Parents need to be very motivated if they want to start instrumental lessons this early. Persuading a three-year-old to practice is not the easiest thing in the world, and supervision and participation are absolutely essential. On the other hand, practice sessions may well turn out to be one of the few things that parent and child can really focus on together, something that interests both of them equally. After all, how much does the average parent really enjoy playing with Ninja Turtles or building with blocks? It is important to be sure that the child really is enjoying it, however.

Many parents prefer not to put the pressure of instrument mastery on a child that early; instead they prefer the Dalcroze- or Orff-type programs, saving formal lessons until the child is six or older.

When it comes to choosing an instrument, look for cues from the child. If she is six, and begging for lessons on the violin, why not let her try? If you need to make the suggestion, try and sense what sort of musical sounds appeal to her, and help her pick the instrument accordingly. The Swiss oboist, composer, and conductor Heinz Holliger believes that children are naturally inclined to particular instruments, and training on the wrong one can stifle a child's musical impulses. For help in deciding, you could investigate your local music school: these establishments sometimes have open house events, bringing in players to demonstrate a wide range of instruments and letting children try them out. The piano is a wonderful beginning instrument because of its immense variety. A pianist can play more than one musical line at a time, and because its pitches are fixed, the child can create a beautiful sound more quickly. The piano is also a splendid tool for learning about how music is put together. Most conductors and composers can play the piano at some level. Numerous well-known soloists began their musical lessons on the piano and only later took up the instrument which became their primary focus. If the child starts one instrument and decides that she likes another one better, that should be your cue for a change.

Pianos are expensive, so a parent might consider renting one until it seems certain that the child is really interested and wants to continue. Other instruments may also be available for rental through schools or music stores. One way to experiment with the piano without investing in an actual instrument is by using the Miracle computer software. This package, published by Software Toolworks, comes with an electronic keyboard and can be used with a personal computer or Nintendo setup. It uses a video game format to teach a series of graded piano lessons, and it may be used by children and adults. It does not claim to be a replacement for long-term music lessons, however.

The most important factor to consider when you are looking into music lessons is the teacher. When you choose a teacher, you look for someone who agrees with your ideas for your child's education. I wouldn't look for the teacher whose students win the most competitions or go on to conservatories. If music lessons are supposed to be about exploration and pleasure, about creating a musically literate person who can participate in music in whatever way he likes, you want a teacher who is flexible, sensitive, and creative. Ask her how she teaches, and what her expectations are. Does she have children dance the minuet they are learning and look at pictures of the clothes in which it was danced originally, so that they can physically feel the ordered, formal nature of the piece? Can she guide the child in improvisation? Many terrific teachers can't, of course, but it's something I would like to see, since the creation of art is a powerful means toward the understanding of it. In short, is she teaching music rather than just piano playing?

Different children need different kinds of teachers. Someone who is planning to turn your sensitive eight-year-old into the next Itzhak Perlman (one of the greatest violinists alive today) might be too focused on that goal to pay attention to the wishes and interests of the child. (I don't think that kind of teacher is great for any child, really.) On the other hand, someone who is too relaxed might not give a more easily distracted child the atmosphere of challenge and work in which she will function best.

I can't stress enough the need to find a teacher who both loves music and understands children. You will find that no matter the method—be it Suzuki or anything else—the teacher makes the experience. You may have been a victim of a bad teacher yourself and, as a result, were the sort of child who suffered through piano lessons, never practiced, constantly felt humiliated, and gave up with relief, soured on music. I have a friend who, as a child, tried a number of different instruments. After several years at the piano, his teacher told his parents that he was the least talented child he had ever seen, and the effort should be abandoned. That, I think, is an appalling response. Talent is not the issue—interest is, and this child was interested. A flexible teacher could have found some way to exploit that passion; he could have at least suggested another teacher or avenue for its fulfillment. The object, remember, is not to find potential virtuoso performers—it is to foster the joy of music.

Fortunately, that unperceptive teacher did not get the last word. My friend went on to sing in choirs and study several other instruments. When he was in high school, he founded a youth orchestra in his town so that he could have a place to play bassoon. At his college, which was attached to a conservatory, he kept up all of his musical activities. He's now a lawyer with some musicians and artists as clients, an avid concertgoer, and a board member of a musical organization. Occasionally, he plays the piano.

The teacher cannot do it all, either. Ideally, the teacher will be so inspiring that the child will want to practice, but that is not always the case. You may need to set up a definite schedule, in consultation with the teacher, and monitor or participate in practice. For young children, it may be only a few minutes a day. Children often resist the idea of practice, though they are usually happy to do it once they get started, so I think a little judicious nagging is necessary. My kids used to practice for about half an hour before dinner, which gave them the outdoor time after school that they needed, and a way to focus the extra energy once they came inside. I didn't supervise their practicing, though I'd offer help if they wanted it, but on evenings before their lessons I would ask to hear what they had prepared.

The parent can't be so goal-oriented that it spoils the child's pleasure, however. Let them fool around with the instrument. Improvisation and other seemingly unstructured activities are as important as the technical exercises and learned pieces. To have a child bring you a piece he has written and notated himself seems to me as exciting—if not more—as hearing him play "Twinkle Twinkle," at age four. And if your son wants to put aluminum cans on the piano strings and see how that changes the sound while his friend fools around at the keyboard, let him—composers like George Crumb and John Cage do a lot of that too. I'm all for a healthy balance between disciplined study and wild experimentation.

Just as is the case with preschoolers, seeing a beloved adult take an interest in an activity is a fundamental spur toward success with it. If the parent is too busy, why not ask a grandparent, or another relative who has the time and the inclination? Taking the child to lessons, participating in practice, perhaps taking her to concerts, and just talking about music can create a wonderful bond between generations. Even if a grandparent lives far away, the two can talk on the phone or write letters about music lessons. On the other hand, suffocating the child with attention is counterproductive, and there comes a time when the child will want to do something entirely on his own.

My father was a powerful influence on my own piano study. It was my mother who badgered me to practice, but my shy, gentle father made all my achievements worthwhile. He came to every recital I gave, and he also served as my tryout audience for those traumatic experiences. When my program was just about ready, we'd have a dress rehearsal at home. The piano was at one end of the living room, and my father would arrange the seating audience-style and sit at the other end. I would make a grand entrance from the hall and walk to the piano as he applauded. Then I would perform my pieces as he sat, listening attentively to every note and phrase. When I finished, he applauded and I bowed. I adored my father, and I didn't get to spend all that much time with him, so those "dress rehearsals" were important times for us. When I was older, I was able to return the favor by helping my father memorize lines for all the plays he was in, and I'd go to *his* rehearsals.

I saw some of that closeness repeated in the next generation. I think my son Patrick enjoyed his piano lessons so much because music was something we shared. One of my happiest memories is seeing Patrick, age about thirteen, coming downstairs to my birthday party at Hyannis Port. He was recovering from an illness, but he had planned a surprise for me and he was determined that I would get it. He sat down at the piano and launched into "Satin Doll," a great jazz number, which he had learned especially for the occasion. He realized that the best gift was to show me how much something that mattered to me also mattered to him.

Parents do need to guard against that very natural urge to compete. Think about Little League—parents may *say* that what they want is for Junior to have a social, physical, cooperative experience, but deep down, they are longing to see Junior's team clobber the one from the next town. Music lessons are no stranger to this. Many teachers are hooked into the competition circuit, and they measure some of their own worth in seeing their students do well in these local or statewide competitions. Teachers tend to use instruction books that follow a set curriculum, and parents may find themselves measuring their child's progress against another's.

There's nothing inherently wrong with competition, and kids who enjoy it should certainly have the opportunity. But parents should remember that children learn and absorb at different rates, and they enjoy different things. Learning in the arts is personal above all. One child may thrive on getting piece after piece perfect; another may learn more from writing his own music. But at the same age, they may be expected to compete at the same performance level. Competitions in the professional music world are famous for selecting consensus candidates rather than extraordinary musicians, and competitions on junior levels are certainly not immune. It would be a pity to see a musical, imaginative child discouraged by a poor showing in a competition. And however much the competitive instinct has taken over the professional world, that still is not what music or any of the arts is about. Individual creativity and love for what one is doing, it seems to me, are more important than first prize.

I think that group lessons can be valuable. Just as I always invited my children to bring a buddy when they went to a concert or ballet with me, I think that lessons can benefit from that kind of sharing and camaraderie. Children feel that they're in it together, and just as their imaginations take flight from each other when they play games, so it can happen with music. Even if children don't take their actual lessons together, it's a good idea to have them get together regularly for duo or ensemble playing, and many teachers emphasize this sort of work. My teachers used to have monthly get-togethers at which we would all play, listen to each other, critique, and learn about repertoire. I also remember how thrilling it was to play chamber music when I was an adult, and it is an experience that I think can be splendid for young players as well. Playing together means listening to the other person, learning to synchronize rhythm, dynamics, and emotion, and creating a splendid sound that is far greater than the sum of its parts. It also builds skills of cooperation and patience.

There's a lot to be said for recitals as well. The shaking knees and clammy hands that I associate with the ones of my own childhood are not my greatest memories, but playing in public never killed me, and the occasional pressure to actually finish something and share it with other people can be galvanizing. I certainly was always very proud when I finished. Little, informal gatherings of students, parents, and friends playing for each other are probably the nicest.

Teaching that includes improvisation and other sorts of "fooling around" as well as theory, music history, and literature may take longer to show concrete results, but I think it sows the seeds for a more complete understanding of music. Once you learn to read, you can read any kind of book, and with a broad grounding in the fundamentals and literature of music, you can enjoy the same range in that field. What is more, expression and communication are, after all, what music is all about. Playing an instrument is a vehicle for interpreting the creations of others, but if you are playing your own creations as well, how much more valuable the experience will be! Teachers of disturbed and disabled children often use the arts as a means for expression, since these are people who really have no other way of communicating. Why should it not be open to all of us?

Think of your average fuming, inarticulate young adolescent. Gunther Schuller's work with narration, *Journey into Jazz,* is all about just such a boy discovering that the trumpet he has been diligently practicing for so many years is really his voice. The child who has been obediently learning minuets for years may come to adolescence, decide that studying an instrument has nothing to do with his life, and drop the whole thing. It almost happened to me, and I bless my mother for realizing what was happening and turning me over to a new, young teacher who taught me to play popular songs which I could play for my friends at parties. Then, by the time I got to college, and I was ready to tackle other kinds of music, I still had the piano under my fingers. I hadn't given up in disgust, and even though I never became a professional, nor had any desire to do so, I still had—and continue to have—the pleasure of my instrument.

Some parents are delighted to see their child taking an early interest in music, but when interest turns into passion, they despair. They look at their avid young violinist (especially if it's a boy), think "starving musician," and try to divert him to sports or computers. It is true that few musicians make superstar livings, but there are many opportuni-

ties apart from the star soloist or conductor. Orchestra players often make generous livings, as do teachers—and being a
great music teacher is at least as noble a goal as being a
superstar. Chamber musicians, composers, arrangers, solo
artists on the less than superstar level—all of these people
can live nicely, doing what they enjoy. Even if music performing eventually becomes an avocation, as it did for me,
rather than a vocation, there are many ways to make a living
within the musical establishment.

An extremely gifted child makes her own rules, and if you
have one, you'll soon know. That doesn't mean that you
should turn her over to a slave driver, because that is probably the quickest way to crush her spark. Just make sure the
teacher is challenging her at every level, and as soon as that
isn't happening, move on. The teacher may even be the one
to suggest a change. Precollege divisions at conservatories
specialize in talented students and feature orchestra and
other ensemble experiences.

One word about conservatories. If your child is truly
gifted and wants to make music her profession, the conservatory—a school of music that offers a bachelor's or sometimes
graduate degree in music—can be a wonderful place to develop that talent. Many of the best teachers are associated
with them, and music is in the air. There are a handful of
famous ones: The Juilliard School, the Manhattan School,
and the Mannes College of Music in New York City; the
Curtis Institute in Philadelphia; the Eastman School in
Rochester, New York; the Oberlin Conservatory in Oberlin,
Ohio; the San Francisco Conservatory; Boston's New England Conservatory; and the Cleveland Institute.

Conservatories, however, like their horticultural name-
sakes, are hothouses. Many try to offer some kind of liberal
arts curriculum, but for the most part, students there tend to
spend most of their time obsessively working alone in their

practice rooms. An alternative, for a music student who is interested in matters other than music, is the music department of a university. Some, like the School of Music at Indiana University, or the Oberlin Conservatory—which is part of a small, liberal arts college—are famous in their own right and have excellent teachers and musical opportunities while offering at least the possibility of a liberal education. My friend Yo-Yo Ma, already marked for greatness in his teens, decided to attend Harvard rather than a conservatory because he wanted to study more than just the cello. It took him a lot of work to graduate, but he has never regretted it.

Studying music as a child certainly can't hurt, if properly done, but if it doesn't take, so be it. If the child really hates the lessons, and it's not just a mismatch with instrument or teacher, then let it go. Perhaps he would be happier dancing, drawing, writing, or learning about computers. Kara dropped piano when she became passionately interested in sports. Not everybody likes music—I just think they should have the opportunity to find out if they do. My son Teddy, who took piano lessons for a while, told me recently, "I never practiced, or else I practiced for half an hour before I went for a lesson, and my teachers knew it. You regret once you're older not having spent more time doing it, but it takes a lot of time and discipline, and when you're growing up, there are so many other interests, like sports, that seem much more important at the time. Your parents tell you that you'll appreciate the time spent on music when you're older, but of course you don't realize that *until* you're older. I can say that as a listener, the piano has always been my favorite instrument."

Music lessons are not just for kids or professionals, however. There's nothing that says that the adult who suffered through piano lessons as a child, quit, and now feels a profound sense of opportunities missed doesn't have another chance. Many teachers now specialize in adult beginners, or advanced beginners. I recently did some research for another friend, a high-powered executive who was teaching himself piano and wanted a coach. I looked for someone young and flexible who would incorporate popular music and different kinds of keyboard styles. The young man I found came to his student's home in the evening, rather like a personal trainer. Several of my friends have begun piano lessons as adults and found that the year or two of lessons they had when they were children were by no means wasted. It was like riding a bicycle—suddenly, it all came back.

If you do decide to take lessons, you need to be as clear about your own goals as you are about your goals for your child, and choose a teacher accordingly. Think about issues like the kind of music you'd like to play, how much time you're willing or able to devote to practice, and whether you'd like to play with other people. Adults, remember, have the intellectual advantage over children, but they have lost some of the natural, unquestioning ability to just pick things up. An adult beginner might find playing a different line with each hand at the piano absolutely baffling; a child finds it quite normal. Also, adults have heard a lot more music; they are more likely to compare their own efforts to those of the professionals to whom they've been listening and get discouraged. They are also less open to improvisation and experimentation. And they don't have much time.

If you can see past these hurdles, however, learning an instrument as an adult is a splendid thing. It confers a wonderfully heady sense of mastery. It is something you choose, something that has nothing to do with your job or other day-to-day obligations. It opens up possibilities for expression, and for ensemble playing and performance—all such valuable things in this age of insularity, when people work like demons and then sit exhausted and comatose in front of their television sets.

Even the lessons themselves can be a mind opener. When I went back to school at Lesley College in Boston for my education degree, I started taking piano lessons at the Longy School in Cambridge, Massachusetts. I hadn't had real piano lessons since I graduated from college more than twenty years before, and I wanted to get back that feeling of starting from scratch, to start thinking about what I was doing again. My teacher was a sensitive, gifted young woman who could always figure out something to do with me. If I went in without having practiced, she might give me hints on how to memorize music, or we might just talk about music, both emotionally and theoretically. Sometimes she played pieces for me, things that I might want to work on later. She also played music that had been *written* since I left college. In those days, no student ever played anything that had been written since Debussy, so we never learned to become comfortable with the huge range of styles and techniques that populate this century, either as players or as listeners.

(I don't think matters have improved all that much. When I took a course in contemporary music at the New England Conservatory a few years ago, I found that the college students in the class were as much in the dark about contemporary composition as I was. I think that instrumental lessons can be an intriguing way to find out about music written in this century and what makes those composers tick. A lot of them are my contemporaries. Surely they are saying something that has some resonance with my own life experience!)

If you already have some proficiency in singing or playing and would like to get back into playing in a group, there are many possible avenues. For chamber music, the Amateur Chamber Music Players (which can be reached through Chamber Music America in New York City. See page 203) maintains a list of members all over the country, self-graded as to ability, who are interested in playing with other amateurs. There are a number of summer programs, too, that send adult chamber music aficionados to "camp" for a few weeks.

For larger ensembles, a community orchestra or chorus, fielded by the community music school, or some other entity may be just the thing. Plenty of towns have so-called "doctors' orchestras" (doctors seem to be among the most enthusiastic amateur musicians), with evening rehearsal hours to accommodate work schedules. I remember how my father loved his acting, the release that it gave him, and how proud we always were of him.

Ensemble performing has many of the same pleasures for adults that it has for children. I remember the pleasure of sitting in the orchestra, being part of that sound, the excitement of preparation, the long rehearsals, the delight of the audience at the performances. For adults, ensemble work has extra benefits too. For a change, one is not competing, but working with other people to create something beautiful, whether it's a string quartet or a huge Bach chorus. And there is nothing quite as heady, as guaranteed to make the stresses of ordinary life slip away, as going to that rehearsal, and then getting up on that stage with people you've been working with and giving an audience the best you have.

TEN

A Call to Action

LAST CHRISTMAS, I went to hear Bach's *Christmas Oratorio* at Emmanuel Church in Boston. The *Christmas Oratorio* is an exquisite, gentle work, filled with the humanity and grace of the holiday it celebrates. I closed my eyes and concentrated hard. I could hear the pure lines of the soloists twisting around those of the orchestra, the musical setting making clear the words of the old story. The quiet sinfonia, evoking the music of the shepherds in their fields, gave way to the exultant chorale "Break out, O beauteous morning light!" Suddenly, I felt as though the chorus was singing my own thoughts, my own feelings of peace and exultation at that beautiful season. In the heart of that sacred work, written centuries ago, I heard an echo of my own voice.

I guess I could say the same thing about much of the music I listen to. The gospel singers who sang, clapped, and banged their tambourines at Kara's wedding, the beautiful cello solo at the beginning of the slow movement of Schubert's E-flat Piano Trio, the monumental force and orchestral color of Wagner's operas, the heartbreak of the crippled jester in Verdi's *Rigoletto*—it's all about sorrow and celebration. I listen to it with my mind and with my heart. I can hear how Beethoven took a theme and transmuted it into a gigantic symphonic movement, but what that all comes down to is the connection that he and other composers make with me. They're speaking of my world, and another as well, offering me a glimpse into someone else's imagination. Music is different from words and pictures. I can get carried away by plays and paintings too, but music has a physical and emotional component that goes beyond those arts. Those old church composers knew what they were doing. They were firing up their congregations with music.

I think this connection is something that Americans have lost. Somewhere along the way we started to think that music, along with the other arts, is a frill. It may have something to do with American practicality and utilitarianism, an attitude that has affected so many disciplines. Science and mathematics have become ways to "beat the Russians" (in the fifties) or the Japanese (today); reading and writing are important only because service-oriented corporations need a skilled work force. With such an attitude, the *pleasure* of scientific exploration or even reading books is discounted.

With science and reading turned into strictly "useful" functions, what hope is there for music? One can make utilitarian arguments for the arts, of course, but their centrality has more to do with intangibles like the life of the mind and the life of the spirit. Today's practical, hardworking people are uncomfortable with such things, although we are the ones who need them most. I think President John Adams would be very depressed to see that, two hundred years after he wrote his prediction, we have still not allowed our children—or ourselves—to study music, poetry, and painting.

What is to be done about this? In this book, I have offered suggestions about what parents can do as individuals to rekindle this lost flame for themselves and their children. But as I learned after many years in politics, there is power in numbers, and I believe that people who care about these issues can band together and have an effect where it will make an even larger difference—in the schools.

Music is disappearing from American public schools. With the idea that music is a frill now firmly entrenched, twenty years of budget cutting has resulted in a precipitous drop in the number of specialist music teachers. The active music program in the affluent Boston school district where I did my practice teaching is the exception rather than the rule. Training for elementary school classroom teachers does not include music. This results in schools with no music instruction, instrument lessons, chorus, orchestra, or school musical. In New York City, America's arts capital, where music education is mandated by the state (as it is in many states), two thirds of the public elementary schools have no music or art programs at all, and middle schools and high schools are pretty much unable to fulfill state requirements with the staff they have. Where music does exist in the United States, it is often shifted into so-called "magnet" schools, which provide instruction only for the musically gifted, thereby reinforcing the false idea that music is only for those "in the know."

The result? The creation of a new generation of Americans who know little or nothing about a vital facet of their cultural heritage. Alienated, they do not sing or play instruments. They do not go to symphony concerts or ballet performances or operas or jazz concerts, and the ever aging audiences at these institutions become ever shrinking elites. Most Americans rely for stimulation on the easily grasped, lowest-common-denominator appeal of throwaway mass culture. They can't listen to anything that lasts longer than two minutes unless it has visual accompaniment. They forget the pleasure of the quiet sound in the thrill of the earsplitting one. They are shortchanged, and it's a shame.

We can do something about this. It is up to parents and others who care about music to act, and in schools, parents have power. I spent twenty years in politics, and if I learned anything, it is that politics is the art of persuasion, about swaying large numbers of people to your cause, about getting measures passed against opposition of all stripes. I watched the Kennedys persuade and be persuaded all those years, and I watch my son Patrick doing it now in the Rhode Island legislature. The political idealism of the 1960s is hard to find these days, but I believe that the basic principles, harnessed to something of value, can still re-create that old liberal spirit of inclusion, of voices heard and taken into account, of changes made.

The first step is finding out what your school has. Many school districts still require music, but it may consist of twenty minutes a week, with the singing of the national anthem taking up five of those! Your school may have a dedicated but overworked and burned-out music teacher who meets hundreds of students and doesn't have enough time to devote to any of them.

Go to Back-to-School Night and find out who's teaching music and how—or find someone who would like to include it. There may be a classroom teacher who cares passionately about music, or, in junior high and high school grades, a teacher of some other subject to whom music means a great deal, or even the principal. These are the people who will be on the front lines with whatever program is eventually in place, and their support is key. Let them know that music matters to you, and that you want to help. Whether it's being a teacher's aide for a concert trip, starting an after-school chorus, mobilizing the community to launch a music program, hiring the teachers and designing the curriculum, or setting up an endowment to keep it going, your contribution counts.

The next step is getting people on your side. Find like-minded parents in your children's classes, or in other grades. Parents whose children are just starting school tend to be the most interested, eager, and prepared to take a hand in their education—so look around the kindergarten and first and second grades. Perhaps you've met people with children from your school at youth concerts. Ask the school teacher, or some of the local music teachers, for names of parents who might be interested.

Get them together. When I think back on those innumerable coffees and teas that I attended in my role as a political wife, I realize that they were all about fostering a sense of community while rallying around a cause. People who met the candidate's wife, watched home movies of his kids—we used to show our films of Kara playing with Jack's daughter Caroline—or gave him a dollar had a vested interest in seeing him win, so instead of staying home on Election Day, they would go out and vote. An afternoon open house, or a cocktail party to which you invite the conductor of the orchestra, a few of the players, or a local chamber ensemble, can have the same effect. People persuade where abstractions cannot, and having a living exponent of the art you are trying to foster rubbing elbows with the people whose help you need is a bonus. The musicians can talk about what they do and how they feel about it. Perhaps they will also agree to play something short just to get your guests into the spirit. Gather your volunteers from those who seem most enthusiastic.

The next step is to determine the way that music can best

be integrated into your school program—what is ideal, and what is possible. There are all sorts of avenues. In the elementary school, a general music curriculum, based on techniques such as the Orff and Kodály approaches which I discussed in Chapter Nine (there are many others), and which teaches basic music literacy, listening, history, and performance, building from grade to grade (just as students are taught reading, writing, and arithmetic), is ideal. Some schools offer beginning instrumental instruction. Instrumental and vocal ensembles often take over in the higher grades. Some schools have begun to include chamber music, which is more difficult to supervise than larger group activities but is tremendously rewarding for the students. Some schools reserve ensemble activities for after the regular school day; others can integrate them more easily into the curriculum.

In practice, the general music curriculum may break down into twenty minutes of rote-learned singing once every two weeks, or a session of drawing pictures to music—practices that don't help music to be regarded as something other than a frill. The marching band, if it exists, may be a slave to the band leader's desire to look good on the football field, and the chorus merely an older version of the rote classroom learning of songs in the earlier grades, with uninspiring repertoire. (Why not incorporate sight-singing lessons, for example?) Clearly in these sorts of cases, some kind of augmentation and rethinking could be extremely valuable.

When there is no music teacher, or the one that is there could clearly use some help, consider tapping the valuable resources that already exist in the community and that have a burning interest in getting music into the schools—the local cultural institutions. For years, these orchestras, opera companies, presenters, chamber ensembles, dance groups, and others merely paid lip service to education. They offered the occasional children's concert or opera, often with little preparation for teacher or student. Today, as they see their audiences aging and dwindling, many of them have finally woken up to the importance of music education. They have also discovered that their funding sources are interested in projects that stress education. As a result, in cities all over the United States, arts institutions are going into partnership with schools in new and creative ways, establishing long-term, multifaceted programs that do far more than simply sit children in an audience for an hour a year.

In a program put together by the San Francisco Symphony, students explored the mixed cultures of the Bay Area —black, Hispanic, and Asian—through ethnic music, and then studied the influences of those cultures on European and American classical composers. The Milwaukee Symphony has launched a citywide program, beginning with kindergarten and adding a grade a year so as to eventually cover grades K–12, ensuring continual, sequential learning. Chamber music groups establish long-term residencies in particular schools, meeting the same children in grade after grade, in small groups, and teaching basic musical principles as well as performing. The Chicago Symphony recently used its composer-in-residence in a school project that stressed the writing of music.

Arts institutions are a tremendous resource: children can see the results of what they are learning. The classroom is tied to the real world; they can meet the musicians who play the violin and the timpani in their classrooms, and then see them onstage in the concert hall. They can see close up how the French horn player gets red in the face with the effort required to blow air through those long coils of tubing without having the notes crack; they can feel the physical effort that it takes to stand up supporting the double bass and using the bow to get sounds out of those long strings. When children see people making music and hear them talking, music becomes a part of daily life, not a special, alien, one-time-only event to which they are dragged. Music performed by people is not an abstraction—something complicated and unknowable that comes out of the stereo speakers—but rather something that real people do, make a living at, and love.

Artists, too, can make wonderful teachers. Classroom teachers may have lost the spark that brought them to their subject in the first place, but for an artist, that spark is his life. Having learned techniques for communicating with words as well as with voice or instrument, that artist can be an especially eloquent spokesman, rekindling his own enthusiasm in his students.

Education has lately become a popular cause for funders. With corporations and foundations now interested in targeting their money in this way, cultural institutions should be even more receptive to parents who are eager to help them form partnerships with schools. Some research into the funding patterns of your local orchestra, opera company, or ballet company might yield some valuable ideas about how to make your agendas dovetail.

Making contact with the cultural organization is not difficult. Networking, if possible, is a useful first step. Is one of the parents in your group on the board of directors, or friendly with someone who is? Is anyone acquainted with a symphony staff member (if that is the group you are planning to approach)? If none of these approaches are feasible, simply contact the education director or coordinator. If the organization is too small to have someone with that title, contact the executive director, and/or find out who has education responsibilities in the organization.

The cultural institution may already have a program in the works, or it may be interested in starting one. Should the staff members feel they need some outside suggesting in how to set up a successful partnership, there are a number of national consultants who work in this area. Another community resource is the local college, university, or conservatory, which may have a music education program or a chamber-ensemble-in-residence. Some cities also have central clearinghouses for cultural programs that are offered to schools.

With the orchestra or other institution interested, you will need to get your school to cooperate and work with the cultural organization in determining what the program will be, how it will be organized, and who will pay for it. Along with your core of parents, you should also enlist the aid and interest of the school music teacher, if there is one, and the principal, if you have not already done so.

Never underestimate the power of the Parent-Teacher Association. Interested PTAs run schools—school boards are entirely parent-driven. So get your lobby together, and use the PTA as your arena.

I watched lobbyists and politicians for twenty years, but I also saw an extremely effective campaign for in-school music mounted through a PTA. When I did my practice teaching in a public elementary school in Brookline, Massachusetts, in 1979, some parents got together to institute after-school activities there. It was a powerful lesson in the techniques—and frustrations—of grass-roots politics.

Just to get the school to stay open for one afternoon a week, from 3 P.M. to 5 P.M., required tremendous mobilization and persuasion. Teachers and custodians had to be paid to stay later. Was that money well spent? Where would it come from? Bus schedules had to be changed. Some parents wanted extra time devoted to sports, so the culturally oriented parents did a lot of horse trading—a sports activity for a cultural one. It reminded me of the way congressmen get their special projects passed by attaching riders to bills that have broad support. Sports enthusiasts are legion: why not harness their energies to your campaign?

It took several years to get that afternoon in Brookline together. It took time to persuade parents to join the effort. Big school activities, like the all-school musical in December, got more people interested. When they saw their children involved in everything from playing in the orchestra to painting the sets, they were more likely to sign petitions, show up at board meetings, and volunteer to help with time or money.

Your local cultural institution partner can also help persuade large numbers of parents to participate. Some will organize informal musical events, geared to families, which show the kinds of learning that will be taking place in the classroom. Some even sponsor education programs for parents that parallel what their children will be learning in school. And as adults feel increasingly secure about their knowledge of the field, they begin to see their children's education in it as having greater value. Music also becomes something in which they can participate with their children, and children and parents can act as models for each other.

Parents who become school activists quickly discover a basic principle that every politician knows—the squeaky wheel gets the grease. People who are vocal and emphatic get attention. The polite, self-effacing person who merely asks, "Please do this for me" and assumes that, because his mission is right, it will be valued will probably not get very far. At budget meetings, in which everyone yells for his particular piece of the pie, the recluse will not be heard. Personal diplomacy and compromise are also valuable tools for the activist. And if you need help with any step of the process, state and local legislators know how these things are done, and they are useful resources.

If your school holds out against the idea of paying a music teacher, or enough music teachers, music can still be integrated creatively into the curriculum using outside "experts" (artists) as long as there is some sort of training component for the classroom teacher who really carries the ball. Music can be the glue that holds different subjects together, and teachers are longing for such handles on material. A program built around song, for example, could incorporate actual singing, which is a basic musical skill, and the musical analysis of how songs are put together, but also the study of texts of songs (poetry of different kinds), their historical background and social context, and scientific principles of biology (vocal production) and acoustics. Children read, write, sing, and compose, as well as hearing professional singers of different genres, including classical and folk of whatever kind is available in the community. How does the vocal production of a singer of traditional Chinese music, for example, compare with that of a Latin-American folk artist, or an opera singer?

One essential ingredient in the process is the teacher—music specialist or otherwise—who will be welcoming this program into his or her classroom. Well-meaning parents may band together to pay for a presentation in the school, only to find that the teachers know nothing about it, find it an intrusion, and are therefore unsupportive. The result is that the students troop into a large assembly, having only been told, "I don't know what this is, but please be quiet." An enriched program that dovetails creatively with the teacher's own needs is far more likely to be a success.

This kind of music education requires effort. It's a lot easier to put a record on the turntable and have the children draw pictures. But that is the kind of "music appreciation" that has given the field a bad name and, worse yet, made it seem expendable. Imagine, instead, a training orchestra of young musicians that comes into an elementary school, has its audience seated in and around the players, stops frequently to answer questions, and has the students who persist in opening and closing the Velcro straps on their sneakers do it on cue, as part of the music. Or a teacher who begins teaching basic listening by asking the children to listen—to nothing in particular—for fifteen seconds, and then talk about what they heard. Or a class given over to student chamber ensembles who learn to resolve differences, listen to themselves and each other, and create something without the direction of some authority figure.

In my ideal world, all children would study music in school as they study reading. They would be taught by inspired, dedicated teachers who loved and understood their subject, who would awaken interest and fire the imagination of children. Even if all this didn't produce music-loving adults, the children who had that education would at least have had the opportunity to find out that it was there.

The ideal world, of course, is just that. Great teachers and great music programs exist, but for the rest, we need to struggle ahead and better what we have. Just getting the mechanism for learning about music in place puts us ahead of the game. It seems to me that there must be something for today's children, something that will spur the life of the imagination. I'm not interested in creating a universe of piano virtuosos, just a world filled with people who aren't afraid to listen or sing.

ELEVEN

Postscript

I'VE BEEN LIVING in Boston for more than ten years now, and much of my public and private life centers on music. Every year, I host a benefit for a mental health clinic at the Boston Pops. I take my friends to concerts, ballets, and operas, and they take me. I keep up with my musician friends, go to their performances, delight in their triumphs. In May 1991, I went to the all-day gala concert that capped Carnegie Hall's centennial season in New York, and I reveled in Yo-Yo Ma and Isaac Stern's performance of Brahms' Double Concerto.

I still listen to music at home almost constantly, and I have different favorites for different times of day. In the morning, for example, I'll play vocal music, like Leontyne Price singing Verdi or Puccini arias, to wake me up. Symphonies are for the afternoon, and chamber music for late at night, my favorite time of day, when I'm sitting up reading. Sometimes

I give the music my full attention; at other times, it is a background for my activities. I'm still passing out recordings, too. When I stay with friends, I bring along a few CDs as a gift (since Lenny Bernstein died, I've been bringing his music a lot), and some musical toys or books (sometimes the ones with little keyboards) for the children, some of whom are starting to refer to me as "the lady who brings music."

The piano is in my living room, and I work at it sporadically, trying out an old piece I haven't thought about for years (a little Bach, perhaps) or fooling around with something new. I get lost in that musical world, trying to make the notes and phrases come out the way I want them. When I've been away for a few weeks, with no piano at all, I'll sit down in front of it for fifteen minutes and wonder if I still remember how to play, if my fingers can still make the sounds I hear in my head. The wonderful thing is that even though those sessions start out haltingly, the fluency comes back. It's always exciting to find that it didn't go away, that I can keep it and enjoy it anytime I like.

Occasionally, I'll accept an invitation to perform for a charity, and then I have to work in a more serious, concentrated way. I try mentally to put myself back into that little cubicle at Manhattanville College, during that spring when I was preparing for my senior recital. But I'm not twenty-one anymore, and I'm no longer capable of the sustained concentration required for day in, day out immersion in music. Now, I have to change my habits entirely: say no to social engagements, turn off the phone, and get to bed early (that's the real sacrifice; I'm a night person) so that I can get my mind, spirit, and fingers in shape for a concert. I have to spend months reestablishing my technique. I can work intensively for only an hour and a half or so, and then I have to stop; I'll go for a run up the Charles River or just take a walk and clear my head.

It's grueling, but it's exciting, a bit like getting back to my first fresh days in politics. The paring down of my life is exhilarating, and for a few months, I know once again what it tastes like to be totally devoted to music. That's part of the reason that I love professional musicians so much: I've had, however briefly, a bit of the experience that they live with. And I know what it takes to get just to the point where you can technically conquer your instrument, and how infinitely greater is the leap beyond, when you put your heart and soul at the service of your art.

I'm a true amateur, I guess. The word comes from the Latin meaning "to love." The point is not that I play exceptionally well, or all the time, or professionally—which I don't—but rather that I know what goes into doing those things, and that once in a while, I will get to work, out of love.

In the last few years, I have had the joy of seeing people I love come to music, too. My daughter Kara, who gave up piano lessons in favor of sports nearly twenty years ago, is a case in point. While she lived in Boston, she worked as a producer for our NBC-TV affiliate station. One of the last stories she did there was a profile of Doriot Anthony Dwyer, the principal flutist of the Boston Symphony, who was ending her long tenure with the orchestra by performing the world premiere of a concerto that had been written for her by Ellen Taaffe Zwilich, one of America's most prominent composers and a woman to boot. Kara chose that story for both its feminist and musical angles, and she called me for a little advice when she began to work on it. Kara says, "I wasn't quite sure about the difference between a concerto and other kinds of pieces, and I wanted to ask intelligent questions."

Kara filmed the flutist teaching, rehearsing, and finally performing. I had tickets to the concert, and as Dwyer played the concerto, I could watch her and see my daughter directing the cameramen to capture the experience on film. Later, when we went backstage, Doriot Anthony Dwyer told me how professional and intelligent my daughter was, and that she was thrilled with Kara's interview because she gives better interviews when the questions are good. It was a night for feminine and filial pride all around.

Kara lives in Washington now, where she is producer and video coordinator for Very Special Arts, which provides education and training through the arts for people with disabilities. After all these years, the arts have become central to her life, as they are to mine, and I can't help but feel a wonderful kind of completion and continuity in it all.

I've gone on with my own explorations as well. The experience of discovering gospel music for Kara's wedding was so exciting that I thought it might be fun to find out about another kind of music that was fairly new to me. I also wanted to practice what I'm preaching, to re-create for myself the methods that I'm advocating in this book. So I decided to find out more about jazz.

I talked to friends, like the disc jockey Ron Della Chiesa at Boston's public radio station, and the composer-conductor Gunther Schuller, who are jazz experts. I started going to some concerts. Summertime is great for jazz, and Boston is packed with possibilities, many of them free. One night, I tried out Boston's Jazz Boat, which does evening cruises around Boston Harbor. That night I heard an amateur group, the Black Eagle Jazz Band, which is a bunch of doctors on sax, trumpet, piano, bass, and drums. These guys make plenty of money in their regular profession, but they reserve hunks of their minimal free time to rehearse their music and perform around town because they love it so much. I loved it too. I responded instantly to jazz; its swing, its freedom of improvisation, of never quite knowing who's going to take off next, and in what direction—a freedom that keeps not only the musicians but the audience on the hop. I loved the emphasis on rhythm, the twisting and turning of standard tunes every which way until every facet sparkled and shone. I loved the solo flights of improvisation, and the moment of truth as all the instruments joined together again.

My own "journey into jazz" hasn't been a piece of cake, however. Whenever I start something new, I feel that I have to learn everything about it very quickly. So I bought several encyclopedic books and ordered the Smithsonian Institution's *Collection of Classical Jazz,* a book and six-tape introduction to the form, and I started to read and listen. I assumed that I would be able to follow it all because of my musical training, but a lot of the technical explanations baffled me. I'm pretty good at understanding harmony, but rhythm has never really been my strong point, and rhythm is a lot of what jazz is all about—beats that are nothing like classical music, and irregular rhythms that switch from bar to bar. What is more, I found that basic styles and periods are hard to define in jazz. The greatest exponents are both composers and performers, many of whom started out doing one thing and ended up doing something entirely different. Remember Picasso's "Blue Period"? Well, the jazz guys (and they're almost all guys, except some of the singers) have half a dozen periods apiece.

So I stopped trying to intellectualize everything, and I just listened for a while. I found, not surprisingly, that I responded best to the big band sound. It's danceable, and I've certainly danced to lots of big band music in my time, especially in the fifties—I was around for some of the swing era, after all. I especially liked the music of Duke Ellington (1899–1974), partly because he really exploited the big orchestral sound, but especially because he was a pianist and the arrangements let his playing shine as a complement to the whole. I guess my own biases cut across musical genres: I also took to the music of pianists Thelonious Monk (1918–82), who wrote for smaller ensembles, and Cecil Taylor (1933–), a conservatory-trained musician who shows the influence of classical composers in his incredibly energetic music.

After piano, I like saxophone jazz. I find the saxophone a really sexy instrument. It sounds like a man speaking right to me, especially in the lower, growly registers, and I love its extreme dynamic range. I went to hear Sonny Rollins (1929–) in Cambridge and found his music exciting, if sometimes inscrutable. I must admit that when he began playing, I could follow him just fine, but once he started embellishing, he lost me. Indeed, in the jazz I listened to, the pieces I liked best were the ones whose melodies I could hear—which is, I guess, because I'm a beginner.

I found out that jazz suffers from some of the same prejudices people have about classical music. It grew up in New Orleans early in this century as entertainment music, for dancing—and even funerals. In the 1930s and 1940s it *was* America's popular music, a common language. Classical music was once a common language too, when Bach was writing his cantatas, Mozart his concertos, and Chopin his exquisite piano pieces. Now, however, our common language is commercialized pop music, available to all through recordings and radio. No longer a popular form, jazz in some cases has gotten away from its entertainment roots and turned into art music, and some contemporary jazz is as cerebral and challenging to listen to as some contemporary classical music.

Yet if you listen to the recordings of geniuses like Ellington, and some of the young jazz artists on the scene today—like the virtuoso trumpeter Wynton Marsalis—you can't help but be moved and excited by the freedom and inventiveness of their music. Classical composers used to be performers:

Mozart improvised at the keyboard in public all the time. For that eighteenth-century audience, which understood the ins and outs of that musical language, it must have been extraordinary to hear how he could take a tiny theme and invent a whole piece. (If you've seen the movie *Amadeus,* you'll probably remember the scene in which Mozart takes Salieri's little tune and wittily turns it into something much larger—and better.) That's part of the thrill of jazz performance, something that classical musicians left behind when the functions of performer and composer were split.

I'd like to be able to follow jazz improvisations as I can follow a Beethoven symphony, and perhaps if I keep listening and learning, someday I'll be capable of that. But in the meantime, I can just enjoy this splendid music viscerally and emotionally. Now I often listen to jazz instead of opera in the morning, and I take in the occasional concert.

My own explorations have also given me a new respect for people who are just embarking on the discovery of classical music. Learning all about jazz was a lot more difficult than I thought it would be, and I can now really sympathize with the bafflement of a novice listening to a Beethoven symphony for the first time and trying to read all the books that tell you what to listen for. But I also learned that you don't have to read all the books to get the message, and that ultimately the music is worth the time and effort. I hope you will feel the same way about your discovery of classical music. You don't have to know everything about it to take pleasure in it. Just listen, and enjoy.

APPENDIXES

I Glossary of Terms

ADAGIO (ah-DAH-zho) An Italian tempo designation, meaning "slow" (between andante and largo).

ALLEGRO (ah-LEH-gro) An Italian word designating the tempo (speed) of a piece of music, in this case "fast."

ANDANTE (an-DAHN-tay) An Italian tempo designation, meaning "moderate walking speed" (between allegro and adagio).

BAROQUE (ba-ROKE) Music written during the period of roughly 1600–1750.

CADENZA (cah-DEN-za) A virtuosic solo passage within a larger work, improvised in times past.

CHAMBER MUSIC Works in which each instrument plays a single musical line without being doubled for a stronger sound. Some traditional groupings are string quartets (two violins, viola, cello), piano trios (piano, violin, cello), and woodwind quintets (flute, clarinet, oboe, bassoon, French horn); composers in the twentieth century have made chamber music combinations of all manner of instruments.

CLASSICISM Music of Haydn, Mozart, Beethoven, and their contemporaries (including some Schubert); roughly 1770–1830.

CONCERTMASTER (also first violinist) Leader of the violin section; plays violin solo passages, represents the orchestra in discussions with the conductor.

CONCERTO (con-CHAIR-toe) Work for solo instrument and ensemble (originally a composition for a group of soloists and ensemble, as in the *Brandenburg Concertos* of Bach).

CONDUCTOR Individual who leads an orchestra or other large ensemble.

FORTE (FOR-tay) An Italian term designating volume, in this case "loud." Gradations of this include "mezzo forte" (somewhat loud) and "fortissimo" (very loud).

KEY The tonal center to which all the notes in the piece are related (A major or C-sharp minor, for example).

LIEDER (LEED-ur) Composed songs, also called art songs. The word means "song" in German and applies especially to nineteenth-century German compositions by such composers as Franz Schubert and Hugo Wolf.

MINIMALISM A twentieth-century compositional style, influenced by music of Africa and the Far East and built on minute changes of rhythm and melody. Principal composers in the style include Philip Glass, Steve Reich, and John Adams.

MOVEMENT Complete section of a composition with a characteristic speed and idea—usually, though not always, separated from other movements by a pause.

OPERA Dramatic work, intended to be staged, for singers, orchestra, and sometimes chorus.

OPUS Literally, "work" or "piece"; followed by a number; a term used to indicate the approximate chronological place of a work within the composer's output (abbreviated Op.).

ORATORIO (or-ah-TORE-ee-oh) Large-scale work, usually with a religious text, for soloists, chorus, and orchestra (Bach's *Christmas Oratorio;* Handel's *Messiah*).

ORCHESTRA An instrumental ensemble in which a number of instruments play each musical line (first violins, second violins, cellos, and so on). Orchestras may be as small as a dozen players or extend to more than one hundred; they may include only strings or have a full complement of wind, brass, and percussion instruments.

PIANO   An Italian volume designation meaning "soft." Gradations include "mezzo piano" (a bit soft) and "pianissimo" (very soft).

PROGRAM   Story or narrative behind a work which may be purely instrumental (Berlioz's *Symphonie fantastique* or Richard Strauss's *Don Juan*).

RECITAL   Concert by an instrumentalist or singer performing alone or (usually) with a piano accompanist.

ROMANTICISM   Musical movement of the nineteenth century. Some composers who have returned to lush tonality in the twentieth century are referred to as "neo-Romantics."

SCORE   Written-out music in all its parts.

SERIALISM   Compositional style based on the twelve-tone process, pioneered by Arnold Schoenberg, which uses a "row" of notes chosen from all twelve steps of the harmonic scale as its basis, rather than the key relationships (A, B-flat, and so on) of traditional tonality. Also called "atonal" and "twelve-tone."

SONATA   Work for solo piano—or other instrument, usually accompanied by piano—usually consisting of three or four movements.

STRING QUARTET   Chamber music grouping of two violins, viola, and cello, and the music written for this type of ensemble.

SYMPHONY   Large-scale work for orchestra, usually in three or more movements.

TEMPO   Speed.

THEME   Starting point or musical idea for a composition. May be an easily identifiable melody.

TONE POEM   A type of nineteenth- or twentieth-century orchestral composition inspired by an extramusical idea; program music. Richard Strauss's *Don Quixote* is one example.

TWELVE-TONE   See serialism.

II   My Favorite Pieces

These are the pieces that I would want on a desert island. They reflect my particular passions; they are, of course, only a minuscule percentage of the music written by each of these composers, and of all the music out there. Start your adventure into music with my choices by all means, but do go on and find your own. Happy listening!

BACH
   Brandenburg Concertos
BEETHOVEN
   Symphony No. 3 in E-flat, *Eroica*
   Symphony No. 6 in F, *Pastoral*
   Symphony No. 9 in D minor, *Choral*
   Piano Concerto No. 3 in C minor
   Piano Sonata No. 14 in C-sharp minor, *Moonlight*
   Piano Sonata No. 23 in F minor, *Appassionata*
BERLIOZ
   Symphonie fantastique
BERNSTEIN
   Fancy Free
   Symphony No. 3, *Kaddish*
   Mass
   West Side Story
BRAHMS
   Symphony No. 1 in C minor

Concerto in D for Violin and Orchestra
Concerto No. 1 in D minor for Piano and Orchestra
Concerto No. 2 in B-flat for Piano and Orchestra

BRITTEN
The Young Person's Guide to the Orchestra

CHOPIN
Everything! All the waltzes, preludes, polonaises, nocturnes, études, ballades, mazurkas . . .

COPLAND
Appalachian Spring
Rodeo
Billy the Kid

DEBUSSY
All the solo piano music (for example, *Arabesques, Children's Corner, Clair de lune*)
Images (for orchestra)
La Mer
Prelude à l'après-midi d'un faune
String Quartet in G minor

DVOŘÁK
Symphony No. 9 in E minor, *From the New World*
Slavonic Dances
Concerto in B minor for Cello and Orchestra

GRIEG
Peer Gynt Suites No. 1 and 2

HANDEL
Music for the Royal Fireworks
Water Music
Messiah

HAYDN
Symphonies No. 93–104, *London Symphonies*
Quartet in D, Op. 64, No. 5, *The Lark*
Quartet in C, Op. 76, No. 3, *Emperor*

LISZT

Sonata in B minor for Piano

MAHLER

Symphony No. 5 in C-sharp minor

MOZART

Symphony No. 41 in C, K. 551, *Jupiter*
Concerto No. 21 in C for Piano and Orchestra, K. 467

PROKOFIEV

Peter and the Wolf

PUCCINI

La Bohème, Madama Butterfly (operas)

RACHMANINOFF

Rhapsody on a Theme of Paganini for piano and orchestra
All four piano concertos
Symphony No. 2 in E minor

RAVEL

Daphnis and Chloe Suites No. 1 and 2

SCHUBERT

Wanderer-Fantasie for piano
Symphony No. 9 in C, *Great*

SCHUMANN

Concerto in A minor for Cello and Orchestra
Concerto in A minor for Piano and Orchestra

SHOSTAKOVICH

Symphony No. 5 in D minor

SIBELIUS

Symphony No. 2 in D

STRAVINSKY

The Firebird
Petrouchka
Rite of Spring
Histoire du soldat

TCHAIKOVSKY

Concerto No. 1 in B-flat minor for Piano and Orchestra

Swan Lake
Concerto in D for Violin and Orchestra
VIVALDI
The Four Seasons
WAGNER
Overtures and preludes to the operas

III Popular Classical Pieces

These are some of the most loved classical works in the repertoire. I've divided them into several categories for easy reference.

ORCHESTRAL/CHORAL

ADAMS, JOHN (1947–)
The Chairman Dances
BACH, JOHANN SEBASTIAN (1685–1750)
Brandenburg Concertos (six), BWV 1046–51
Cantata No. 140, "Wachet auf, ruft uns die Stimme"
Concertos (seven) for harpsichord and orchestra, BWV
1052–58
Concerto for Two Violins and Orchestra, BWV 1043
BARBER, SAMUEL (1910–81)
Adagio for Strings (arranged from String Quartet, Op.
11)
BARTÓK, BÉLA (1881–1945)
Concerto for Orchestra
Music for Strings, Percussion, and Celesta
BEETHOVEN, LUDWIG VAN (1770–1827)
Concerto No. 2 in B-flat for Piano and Orchestra, Op.
19

Concerto No. 3 in C minor for Piano and Orchestra, Op. 37

Concerto No. 5 in E-flat for Piano and Orchestra, Op. 73, *Emperor*

Concerto in D for Violin and Orchestra, Op. 61

Overtures: *Leonore* No. 3; *Egmont*

Symphony No. 5 in C minor, Op. 67

Symphony No. 7 in A, Op. 92

Symphony No. 9 in D minor, Op. 125

BERLIOZ, HECTOR (1803–69)

Symphonie fantastique, Op. 14

BERNSTEIN, LEONARD (1918–90)

Overture to *Candide*

BLOCH, ERNEST (1880–1959)

Schelomo—Hebrew Rhapsody for Cello and Orchestra

BORODIN, ALEXANDER (1833–87)

Polovtzian Dances from *Prince Igor*

BRAHMS, JOHANNES (1833–97)

Academic Festival Overture

Concerto No. 2 in B-flat for Piano and Orchestra, Op. 83

Concerto in D for Violin and Orchestra, Op. 77

Symphony No. 1 in C minor, Op. 68

Symphony No. 2 in D, Op. 73

Symphony No. 4 in E minor, Op. 98

CHOPIN, FRÉDÉRIC (1810–49)

Concerto No. 2 in F minor for Piano and Orchestra, Op. 21

COPLAND, AARON (1900–90)

Appalachian Spring

Fanfare for the Common Man

Rodeo

Symphony No. 3

DEBUSSY, CLAUDE (1862–1918)
Images (for orchestra)
La Mer
Prelude à l'après-midi d'un faune
DVOŘÁK, ANTONÍN (1841–1904)
Carnival Overture
Concerto in B minor for Cello and Orchestra, Op. 104
Symphony No. 8 in G, Op. 88
Symphony No. 9 in E minor, Op. 95, *From the New World*
FAURÉ, GABRIEL (1845–1924)
Requiem, Op. 48
GERSHWIN, GEORGE (1898–1937)
An American in Paris
Rhapsody in Blue
HANDEL, GEORGE FRIDERIC (1685–1759)
Messiah
Music for the Royal Fireworks
Water Music
HAYDN, FRANZ JOSEPH (1732–1809)
Symphony No. 45 in F-sharp minor, *Farewell*
Symphony No. 94 in G, *The Surprise*
Concerto in E-flat for Trumpet and Orchestra
MAHLER, GUSTAV (1860–1911)
Symphony No. 1 in D
Symphony No. 2 in C minor, *Resurrection*
MENDELSSOHN, FELIX (1809–47)
Overtures, including *Hebrides, Calm Sea and Prosperous Voyage, Ruy Blas*
A Midsummer Night's Dream (incidental music)
Concerto in D minor for Violin and Orchestra
Symphony No. 4 in A, Op. 90, *Italian*
MOZART, WOLFGANG AMADEUS (1756–91)
Concerto No. 5 in A for Violin and Orchestra, K. 219

Concerto No. 23 in A for Piano and Orchestra, K. 488

Sinfonia Concertante in E-flat for Violin, Viola, and Orchestra, K. 364

Symphony No. 35 in D, K. 385, *Haffner*

Symphony No. 41 in C, K. 551, *Jupiter*

Requiem, K. 626

Overtures to *The Marriage of Figaro, Così fan tutte, The Magic Flute*

MUSSORGSKY, MODEST (1839–81)

Pictures at an Exhibition

A Night on the Bald Mountain

PROKOFIEV, SERGEI (1891–1953)

Concerto No. 3 in C for Piano and Orchestra, Op. 26

RACHMANINOFF, SERGEI (1873–1943)

Symphony No. 2 in E minor, Op. 27

Concerto No. 2 in C minor for Piano and Orchestra, Op. 18

RAVEL, MAURICE (1875–1937)

Boléro

La Valse

RESPIGHI, OTTORINO (1879–1936)

The Pines of Rome

RIMSKY-KORSAKOV, NIKOLAI (1844–1908)

Scheherazade

ROSSINI, GIOACCHINO (1792–1868)

Overtures to *The Barber of Seville, William Tell, L'Italiana in Algeri, La Gazza ladra* ("The Thieving Magpie")

SCHUBERT, FRANZ (1797–1828)

Symphony No. 8 in B minor, D. 759, *Unfinished*

Symphony No. 9 in C, D. 944, *Great*

SCHUMANN, ROBERT (1810–56)

Concerto in A minor for Piano and Orchestra, Op. 54

Symphony No. 1 in B-flat, Op. 38, *Spring*

SHOSTAKOVICH, DMITRI (1906–75)
  Concerto No. 1 in E-flat for Cello and Orchestra, Op. 107
  Symphony No. 5 in D minor, Op. 47
SIBELIUS, JEAN (1865–1957)
  Concerto in D minor for Violin and Orchestra, Op. 47
  Symphony No. 2 in D, Op. 43
  Finlandia, Op. 26
SMETANA, BEDŘICH (1824–84)
  Overture to *The Bartered Bride*
  Má Vlast (includes *The Moldau*)
STRAUSS, RICHARD (1864–1949)
  Till Eulenspiegels lustige Streiche, Op. 28
  Also sprach Zarathustra, Op. 30
  Four Last Songs
STRAVINSKY, IGOR (1882–1971)
  Rite of Spring
  The Firebird
  Petrouchka
  Pulcinella
TCHAIKOVSKY, PIOTR ILYICH (1840–93)
  Concerto No. 1 in B-flat minor for Piano and Orchestra, Op. 23
  Concerto in D for Violin and Orchestra, Op. 35
  1812 Overture, Op. 49
  Symphony No. 5 in E minor, Op. 64
  Symphony No. 6 in B minor, Op. 74, *Pathétique*
  Italian Capriccio, Op. 45
VERDI, GIUSEPPE (1813–1901)
  Requiem
  Overtures to *La Forza del destino, Luisa Miller*
VIVALDI, ANTONIO (1678–1741)
  The Four Seasons
  Concerto in C for Mandolin and Orchestra, R. 425

WAGNER, RICHARD

Overtures to *Die Meistersinger von Nürnberg, The Flying Dutchman*

Prelude to Act III of *Lohengrin*

"Ride of the Valkyries" from *Die Walküre*

"Good Friday Spell" from *Parsifal*

CHAMBER MUSIC

BARTÓK

Quartet No. 5

BEETHOVEN

Trio No. 4 in D, Op. 70, No. 1, *Ghost*

Trio No. 6 in B-flat, Op. 97, *Archduke*

Quartet No. 9 in C, Op. 59, No. 3

BORODIN

Quartet No. 2 in D

BRAHMS

Quintet in F minor for Piano and Strings, Op. 34

Quartet No. 1 in G minor for Piano and Strings, Op. 25

Quartet in C minor, Op. 51, No. 1

Songs

Liebeslieder waltzes for piano four-hands and voices

DEBUSSY

Quartet in G minor, Op. 10

DVOŘÁK

Trio No. 4 in E, Op. 90, *Dumky*

Quartet No. 12 in F, Op. 96, *The American*

Quintet in A for Piano and Strings, Op. 81

FAURÉ

Quartet No. 1 in C minor for Piano and Strings, Op. 15

KODÁLY, ZOLTÁN (1882–1967)

Duo for Violin and Cello, Op. 7

MESSIAEN, OLIVIER (1908–)
Quartet for the End of Time
MOZART
Quintet in A for Clarinet and Strings, K. 581
Quartet in F for Oboe and Strings, K. 370
Serenade in G, K. 525, *Eine kleine Nachtmusik*
Serenade No. 10 in B-flat for Thirteen Wind Instruments
POULENC, FRANCIS (1899–1963)
Sextet for Piano and Woodwind Quintet
PROKOFIEV
Overture on Hebrew Themes, Op. 34b
RAVEL
Quartet in F for Strings
Trio for Violin, Cello, and Piano
Introduction and Allegro for harp, flute, clarinet, and string quartet
SCHUBERT
Quartet No. 14 in D minor, D. 810, *Death and the Maiden*
Quintet in A for Piano and Strings, D. 667, *Trout*
Piano Trio No. 2 in E-flat, D. 929
Die Winterreise (song cycle); other songs such as "Die Forelle," "Erlkönig," "Du bist die Ruh'," and "Auf dem Wasser zu singen"
SCHUMANN
Quintet in E-flat for Piano and Strings, Op. 44
SHOSTAKOVICH
Quintet in G minor for Piano and Strings, Op. 57
Quartet No. 8 in C minor, Op. 110
SMETANA
Quartet No. 1 in E minor, *From My Life*
TCHAIKOVSKY
Quartet No. 1 in D, Op. 11

WOLF, HUGO (1860–1903)
Italian Serenade for string quartet
Songs, including the *Mörike-Lieder, Italienisches Liederbuch*

SOLO MUSIC AND SONATAS

BACH
Italian Concerto in F for Harpsichord, BWV 971
Suites (six) for unaccompanied cello, BWV 1007–12
Sonatas (three) and partitas (three) for unaccompanied violin, BWV 1001–6

BARTÓK
Romanian Folk Dances for Piano
Sonata for Two Pianos and Percussion

BEETHOVEN
Sonata No. 8 in C minor for Piano, Op. 13, *Pathétique*
Sonata No. 14 in C-sharp minor for Piano, Op. 27, No. 2, *Moonlight*
Sonata No. 23 in F minor for Piano, Op. 57, *Appassionata*
Sonata No. 9 in A for Violin and Piano, Op. 47, *Kreutzer*
Sonata No. 5 in F for Violin and Piano, Op. 24, *Spring*

BRAHMS
Sonatas for Violin and Piano, Op. 78, 100, 108
Sonatas (two) for clarinet and piano, Op. 120
Sonatas (two) for cello and piano, Op. 38, 99

CHOPIN
Ballades, preludes, waltzes, mazurkas

DEBUSSY
Clair de lune
Estampes
Sonata No. 3 in G for Violin and Piano
Sonata No. 1 in D for Cello and Piano

FAURÉ
   Sonata in A for Violin and Piano, Op. 13
FRANCK, CÉSAR (1822–90)
   Sonata in A for Violin and Piano
GRIEG, EDVARD (1843–1907)
   Sonata No. 3 in C minor for Violin and Piano, Op. 45
MENDELSSOHN
   Sonata No. 2 in D for Cello and Piano, Op. 58
MOZART
   Sonata for Violin and Piano, K. 454
POULENC
   Sonata for Flute and Piano
RACHMANINOFF
   Sonata in G minor for Cello and Piano, Op. 19
   Preludes for piano, Op. 23 and 32
RAVEL
   Gaspard de la nuit
SAINT-SAËNS, CAMILLE (1835–1921)
   Sonata No. 1 in D minor for Violin and Piano, Op. 75
SCHUBERT
   Impromptus (eight), D. 899 and 935
   Sonata in A minor for Arpeggione and Piano, D. 821
SCHUMANN
   Carnaval for piano, Op. 9
   Kinderszenen for piano, Op. 15
   Papillons for piano, Op. 2

OPERA

BELLINI, VINCENZO (1801–35)
   Norma
BIZET, GEORGES (1838–75)
   Carmen

DONIZETTI, GAETANO (1797–1848)
Lucia di Lammermoor
The Daughter of the Regiment
GERSHWIN
Porgy and Bess
GOUNOD, CHARLES (1818–93)
Faust
LEHÁR, FRANZ (1870–1948)
The Merry Widow
LEONCAVALLO, RUGGIERO (1857–1919)
Pagliacci
MASCAGNI, PIETRO (1863–1945)
Cavalleria rusticana
MOZART
The Marriage of Figaro
The Magic Flute
Don Giovanni
PUCCINI, GIACOMO (1858–1924)
La Bohème
Tosca
Madama Butterfly
ROSSINI
The Barber of Seville
STRAUSS, JOHANN (1825–99)
Die Fledermaus
STRAUSS, RICHARD
Der Rosenkavalier
VERDI
La Traviata
Rigoletto
Aida
WAGNER
Die Walküre

Tannhäuser
Lohengrin

DANCE

ADAM/PERROT AND CORALLI
Giselle
BERNSTEIN/ROBBINS
Fancy Free
BIZET/BALANCHINE
Symphony in C
CHAUSSON/TUDOR
Lilac Garden
CHOPIN/FOKINE
Les Sylphides
CHOPIN/ROBBINS
Dances at a Gathering
COPLAND/DE MILLE
Rodeo
COPLAND/GRAHAM
Appalachian Spring
LAMB AND HAYDN/THARP
Push Comes to Shove
MINKUS/PETIPA
Don Quixote pas de deux
POULENC/MORRIS
Mort subite
PROKOFIEV/ASHTON, CRANKO, MACMILLAN, others
Romeo and Juliet
SOUSA AND KAY/BALANCHINE
Stars and Stripes
STRAVINSKY/BALANCHINE
Apollo

TCHAIKOVSKY/BALANCHINE
  Serenade
TCHAIKOVSKY/IVANOV, many since
  The Nutcracker
TCHAIKOVSKY/PETIPA and IVANOV
  Swan Lake
Traditional/AILEY
  Revelations

IV Orchestra Seating Chart

Courtesy of the National
Symphony Orchestra,
John F. Kennedy Center,
Washington, D.C.

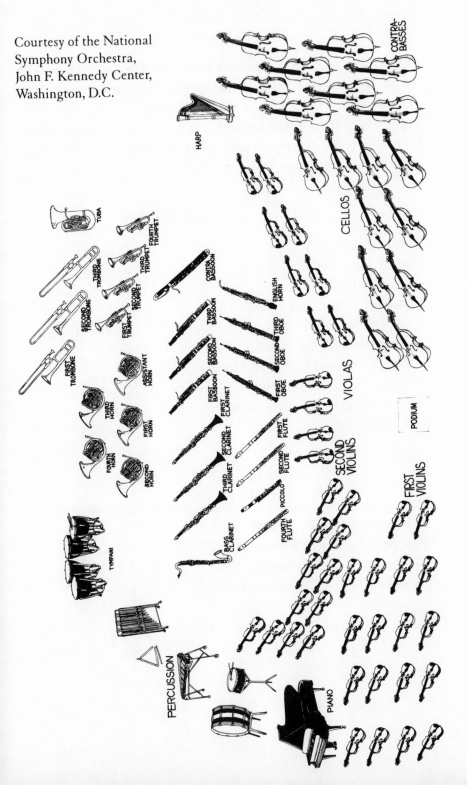

V   Ticket Prices

Concerts of classical music need not be expensive. Here is a list of Boston-area single ticket prices for music and sports events during the 1991–92 season. Remember that the least expensive seat in a concert hall will be far closer to the stage than the least expensive one for a sports event that takes place in an enormous stadium.

MUSIC AND DANCE

Boston Symphony	$19–$52.50
Boston Lyric Opera	$15–$49
Boston Ballet	$11.75–$49.75
Chamber music and recitals	
Symphony Hall	$9.50–$16.50
Museum of Fine Arts	$15
Isabella Stuart Gardner Museum	$6
Boston University School of Music	Free–$5
New England Conservatory	Free
Jordan Hall	$12–$25 (outside groups)

SPORTS

Celtics (basketball), Boston Garden	$12–$31
Red Sox (baseball), Fenway Park	$6–$16
Bruins (hockey), Boston Garden	$16–$39
Patriots (football), Foxboro Stadium	$18–$33

ROCK CONCERTS

Great Woods $12.50–$35
Boston Garden $12.50–$35

VI   Useful Organizations

AMATEUR CHAMBER MUSIC PLAYERS, INC.
  545 8th Ave.
  New York, NY 10018
  212-244-2778
AMERICAN MUSIC CENTER
  30 West 26th St., Suite 1001
  New York, NY 10010-2011
  212-366-5260
AMERICAN SYMPHONY ORCHESTRA LEAGUE
  777 14th St., NW, Suite 500
  Washington, DC 20005
  202-628-0099
ASSOCIATION OF PERFORMING ARTS PRESENTERS
  112 16th St., NW, Suite 620
  Washington, DC 20036
  202-833-2787
CHAMBER MUSIC AMERICA
  545 8th Ave.
  New York, NY 10018
  212-244-2772
DANCE/U.S.A.
  777 14th St., NW
  Washington, DC 20005
  202-628-0144

MUSIC EDUCATORS NATIONAL CONFERENCE
1902 Association Dr.
Reston, VA 22091
703-860-4000
NATIONAL GUILD OF COMMUNITY SCHOOLS OF THE ARTS INC.
PO Box 8018
Englewood, NJ 07631
201-871-3337
SUZUKI ASSOCIATION OF THE AMERICAS
PO Box 354
Muscatine, IA 52761
319-263-3071

Local colleges, universities, concert halls

For more listings, see *Musical America* International Directory of the Performing Arts (annual; available in libraries).

VII   Suggestions for Further Reading

If you're interested in finding out some more about the topics covered in this book, you might want to try the following, available at your local library or bookstore.

ON CLASSICAL MUSIC

Guide to Sonatas and *Guide to Chamber Music* by Melvin Berger (Anchor Books). Both include descriptions of the great works of each genre in nontechnical language.
The Joy of Music by Leonard Bernstein (Fireside Books). The late composer and conductor shares his enthusiasm for music.

What to Listen for in Music by Aaron Copland (W. W. Norton). A wonderful, plainspoken guide for greater appreciation of music by one of America's foremost composers.

Copland on Music by Aaron Copland (New American Library). More thoughts on music from this noted American composer.

An Invitation to the Opera by John Louis DiGaetani (Anchor Books). Introduces opera to the uninitiated.

Inside Music by Karl Haas (Anchor Books). A marvelous, in-depth introduction to all aspects of music by a respected commentator and radio personality.

Beethoven or Bust by David Hurwitz (Anchor Books). A humorous, informative, and easy-to-understand introduction to classical music.

Music in Western Civilization by Paul Henry Lang (W. W. Norton). The classic history, profusely illustrated.

Learn How to Read Music by Howard Shanet (Fireside Books). An introduction to musical notation.

Lectionary of Music by Nicolas Slonimsky (Anchor Books). Full of wit and learning, a reader's encyclopedia of music that's accessible and fun.

ON DANCE

Barefoot to Balanchine by Mary Kerner (Anchor Books). A comprehensive guide to the art of ballet.

How to Enjoy Ballet by Don McDonagh (Doubleday). A wonderful introduction, which is unfortunately out of print—but try your library.

BIOGRAPHIES OF THE COMPOSERS

Johann Sebastian Bach by Werner Felix (W. W. Norton). A recent one-volume biography of this musical giant.

The Life of Ludwig van Beethoven by Alexander W. Thayer, edited by Elliot Forbes (Princeton University Press). While some of the material in this nineteenth-century biography has been superseded by subsequent research, this is still considered by many the finest biography of Beethoven.

Beethoven by Maynard Solomon (Schirmer Books). A recent, more psychological study.

Chopin: The Man and His Music by James G. Huneker (Dover). A solid biography and introduction to this fascinating man and his beguiling music.

Mozart: His Character, His Work by Alfred Einstein (Oxford University Press). A classic biography by the famed musicologist.

Mozart: The Golden Years and *1791: Mozart's Last Year* by H. C. Robbins Landon (Macmillan). While not full biographies, these books are nevertheless marvelous reads and give us a clear-eyed account of Mozart and his times, based on the latest research.

Tchaikovsky by Alexander Poznansky (Schirmer). A new biography, with some bold theories about Tchaikovsky's life and death. More ambitious readers might want to try David Brown's ongoing biography, published by W. W. Norton; three volumes of it have now been published (*Tchaikovsky: The Early Years, 1840–1874; Tchaikovsky: The Crisis Years, 1874–1878; Tchaikovsky: The Years of Wandering, 1878–1885*).

The Lives of the Great Composers by Harold C. Schonberg (W. W. Norton). For those who want to know more about the lives of composers, or who want to get the basics of composers' lives without reading a full-scale biography, this is a marvelous place to start.

FOR CHILDREN

For descriptions, see Chapter Seven.

AGES FOUR TO EIGHT

Voice of the Wood by Claude Clement (Dial Books).
Pet of the Met by Lydia Freeman and Don Freeman (Viking Penguin).
Animal Orchestra by Scott Gustafson (Contemporary Books).
I Like the Music by Leah Komaiko (HarperCollins).
Musical Max by Robert Kraus (Simon & Schuster).

AGES EIGHT AND ABOVE

The Magic Flute by Margaret Greaves (Henry Holt).
Swan Lake by Mark Helprin (Houghton Mifflin).
The Cricket in Times Square by George Selden (Farrar Straus & Giroux, hardcover; Dell, paperback).
Fingers by William Sleator (Bantam).
Ballet Shoes by Noel Streatfeild (Dell).

This is by no means an exhaustive list. Ask your bookseller or librarian about other books related to classical music that you or your children might enjoy.

One Last Note

If you've enjoyed this book and are interested in hearing some of the music I've discussed, you might want to try a special recording, *The Joy of Classical Music* (09026-61378-2/4), produced by RCA Victor as one of the thirty-seven releases in their mid-price Greatest Hits series. With over sixty minutes of music, it contains some of my favorite pieces, including Handel's *Water Music*, Rachmaninoff's *Rhapsody on a Theme of Paganini*, Debussy's *Clair de lune*, and much more. It's available on both CD and cassette at record stores.

INDEX